HOW TO WRITE FOR HOMEMAKERS

THIS IS THE NEW

A DESK BOOK FOR THE PROFESSIONAL HOME
ECONOMIST WHO NEEDS TO COMMUNICATE

A REFERENCE FOR COPYWRITERS, EDITORS,
AND PHOTOGRAPHERS IN HOME ECONOMICS

A TEXTBOOK AND GUIDE FOR STUDENTS
WORKING IN AREAS OF HOME ECONOMICS

A BOOK FOR **YOU**

The Iowa State University Press, Ames, Iowa

HOW TO *Write*

FOR HOMEMAKERS

LOU RICHARDSON

and

GENEVIEVE CALLAHAN

ART BY DON DUDLEY

Composed and printed by
The Iowa State University Press

First edition, 1949
Second printing, 1951

Second edition, 1962
Second printing, 1965
Third printing, 1970
Fourth printing, 1974

Library of Congress Catalog Card Number: 61–14205
International Standard Book Number: 0–8138–0830–8

The Story of This Book

IT ALL STARTED with a discussion of the need of every young home economist for more — and more specialized — training in journalism.

Someone in the group said, "Gen and Lou, you've had journalism courses. You've done magazine editorial work and free-lance writing. Now you are in publicity and advertising, too. Why don't you give a course for those of us who haven't had that kind of training and experience?"

"Well, maybe we might at least have a journalism workshop," we said.

There the idea rested until Marguerite Fenner, chairman of the San Francisco HEIB group at that time, phoned to ask, "What dates do you want to offer that workshop we talked of?"

We hedged. But with Marguerite's gentle persuasion, we set the dates, realizing all too well that the problem was not when and where to give such a workshop, but what to give out in it!

"What," we asked ourselves, "do these young home economists want and need to learn about writing homemaking material? Will they want most help with writing recipes, preparing booklets, writing releases, or setting up photographs? Is it possible to telescope all the subjects asked for into six hours of intensive teaching? How and where can we take hold of the handle?"

These were the questions we turned over in our minds as we studied out what to say and how to say it. Out of that insistent and persistent thinking came the *R/C Formula for Effective Home Economics Communications.* Many of you remember it: *Visualize the Audience. Analyze the Problems. Organize Your Thinking. Dramatize Your Presentation.* This was — and is — the basis of the R/C Workshops in Home Economics Communications.

That first workshop, held in our apartment overlooking San Francisco Bay, bulged the living room walls, but it was enthusiastically received by all who crowded in. Before the series of lessons was over, Corris Guy, then chairman of the Los Angeles group of HEIB, phoned to see if we would give a similar workshop in that city. Then came a letter from Beth Bailey McLean of the Chicago group, emphasizing the need for this type of specialized training and suggesting that we bring the workshop to the Middle West and East. Under the sponsorship of these and other HEIB groups in other cities, we put our workshop on the road.

Among the 150 attending the first Chicago workshop was Kay Goeppinger of the Department of Technical Journalism, Iowa State University. Upon her recommendation, the Iowa State University Press asked that we put our lessons into a book to be called *How To Write for Homemakers.* Thousands of you have owned — and still use — that book. Now, 40 workshops — and several printings — later, it is time for a new edition. And there is more need than ever for the type of information and help contained in it.

How Does the *NEW How To Write for Homemakers* differ from the original? In this important way: The first book was, of necessity, based almost entirely on our own personal experiences. This new edition represents the composite thinking of hundreds of business home economists, home economics teachers, extension specialists, photographers, editors, and copy writers from all over the country.

Those of you who attended one of the earlier workshops will see why and how this pattern evolved. The early workshops, you will recall, were hard-hitting sessions that necessitated copious note-taking. But when the book, *How To Write for Homemakers,* was obtainable, there was less need for taking notes, which meant that more time was available for audience participation. Because all of you were generous about passing along your personal experiences and ideas, the lessons became more valuable, more all-inclusive. The *NEW How To Write for Homemakers* is based on those group discussions. It will, we believe, be a truly useful book for many years to come. A book not only for the home economics student and the young-home-economist-new-on-a-job, but for *all* home economists, and for all editors, copy writers, and photographers who work with home economists. A book for anyone and everyone who hopes to reach homemakers through words and pictures.

And so the story goes from idea to workshop, to book, to book. But this preface would be incomplete without an expression of our personal thanks to all of you who have participated in our workshops and promoted the first edition of this book. Without your coopera-tion and encouragement, the original idea would have remained a conversation piece. The workshops would have begun and ended in our apartment. The first *How To Write for Homemakers* would never have been written, and there would have been no reason for putting out this new edition.

We say to each of you, "This is truly *your book.* Thank you for helping us to make it possible."

Yours for good writing and
greater joy in doing it,

GENEVIEVE CALLAHAN
LOU RICHARDSON

Table of Contents

HOW TO WRITE FOR HOMEMAKERS

1.

Fresh Look at Communications

How to make the most
of words and pictures

ARE YOU a business home economist, a home economics teacher, a home economics student, or a worker in some other phase of home economics education or promotion?

If you are any one of these, you are working in the field of communications. You are communicating your knowledge and skills to homemakers or future homemakers. Or you are learning to do so.

In order to put your ideas across effectively you must recognize one fact right from the start: *all forms of home economics communications involve not merely words but words-and-pictures. The two fit together as neatly and interlock as closely as the two sides of a slide-fastener in a dress!*

This means that every picture you prepare or use must say something. And the words you write or speak must create pictures in the minds of your readers or listeners.

Always keep in mind that everywhere the home-maker or student looks there are pictures. Pictures

In modern communications, words and pictures interlock as closely as the two sides of a slide-fastener.

in newspapers, magazines, and books, on packages and billboards. Living pictures in store displays; lifelike scenes and situations projected on television. Many of these pictures are in direct competition with the messages you hope to put across. The only way you can meet such competition — and thus attract the homemaker or student to your ideas — is to develop picture-mindedness yourself.

This is how it works out.

At times you will be thinking primarily about actual pictures. That is, you will concentrate on a photograph or diagram or display or demonstration or other visual to convey your ideas. But that visual will not be enough. You will still need words to emphasize or expand the idea that is suggested by the visual.

At other times — especially when there are no photographs or other visuals to help you project your idea — you must depend on pictorial words and phrases to create mental pictures.

What do we mean by "pictorial words"? Just this:

When you say that a room is "interesting," you have said nothing. The word "interesting" is meaningless here, because it tells only your personal or subjective reaction to the room. But when you speak of a sun-filled room, or a gay room with living colors, or a cool, quiet room, or an all-family room, you have suggested a picture, and can then fill in with specific details. In such descriptions you have depended on pictorial adjectives.

In other instances you will depend largely on verbs and nouns to inject that pictorial quality. That is, you may say: "Paint the walls with sunshine, using warm yellow paint. Choose open-textured curtains that blend into the sunny-colored walls. Avoid heavy draperies. Use bold-leaved plants for accent."

If you are teaching the fundamentals of room

Writing is a form of communication between two persons — one writer and one reader. It's as simple as that!

Use these marginal areas for your own notes and quotes.

planning, you will probably stress nouns together with the adverbs "why" and "because." As: "These open-textured curtains are a good choice because they filter and soften the light."

If you use a black and white photograph to help in describing the room, you will undoubtedly utilize the caption space to specify colors and tones. If your illustration is in color, the caption space may, instead, call attention to accessories and furniture groupings because the color combination is obvious.

But whether you depend on nouns or adjectives, verbs or adverbs, photographs or no photographs, the ability to substitute pictorial words and phrases for meaningless ones is the trademark of vital communications.

All of us need to work for more of that definitive quality in our writing. Instead of searching for the precise picture-making word to convey our meaning, we are so likely to settle for some worn-out cliché as that word "place." It is one thing to say: "Place the carving knife at the edge of the roast." But when we say: "Place 2 cups of milk or a can of soup in a saucepan," we are being rather ridiculous. What we do is "measure 2 cups of milk," or "empty the can of soup" into the saucepan. More — much more — about words in the chapters that follow.

Another Side of Pictorial Writing

When your copy must run fairly long, as is often the case when writing on practical subjects, work to give those pages pictorial appeal through skillful typographical arrangements. Fiction writers break up pages of solid type by using plenty of short, crisp conversation. You can do it by avoiding long, involved sentences and lengthy paragraphs, and by dropping in well-worded, well-spaced subheads.

WORD TO PONDER

"Empathy" has been defined as the power to move into the life of another person and see with his eyes; feel with his emotions. Although the word is usually associated with fiction writing, it can apply to writing on home subjects, too — family relations, for one example.

Yes, a picture can be worth a thousand words. But it isn't necessary to use a thousand words to project a mental picture. It can be done in a single sentence, sometimes in a single word.

RECIPE WORDS

What recipe words have most appeal for homemakers? One survey shows these topping the list: New; easy; instant; gourmet; protein-packed; low-calorie; family favorites.

But more of all this later on. For the present, establish that picture of the slide-fastener in your mind. Tuck into your Unconscious the thought that words *can* create pictures in the minds of those who see or hear them; that every photograph *can* be a talking picture, saying something worthwhile or interesting. Once you reason in this way, you will find it easier to approach all forms of Home Economics Communications — whether written, spoken, or pictorial.

Now to narrow down your thinking more sharply, and consider that fundamental and frustrating problem — how to get under way.

The Art in This Book

In reading this book, look sharply at the artwork which introduces each chapter. Note that each illustration, together with caption, points up a thought in a way that makes it easy to remember.

"COMMUNICATE" OR "INTERPRET?"

Authors' Note: In this book you will find frequent reference to "Home Economics Communications." Let's look at that phrase.

To "communicate" means not merely to tell, not merely to pass along information and ideas. It involves a two-way process: The giving out of information; and the receiving and understanding of that message.

This means that both sender and receiver must talk and think in the same language. Which, applied to Home Economics Communications, means that the home economist must translate what she has to say into words that will mean something to her particular audience.

Certainly the aim of every home economist is not to stop with the mere feeding of facts, but, rather, to make those facts interesting and digestible. But that aim cannot be attained without an understanding of the principles involved in writing, speaking, and picture-making. This book has to do with those principles.

When, then, you come across the word "communications" in these pages, think of the word not only in its accepted sense, but in its deeper meaning of *interpreting* what you know to those you hope to reach. R/C.

BEWARE THE WEEDS

No homemaker proud of her garden allows it to become choked with weeds. By the same reasoning, no professionally-proud writer permits "weedy," empty words to smother her ideas.

2.

Basic Problem: Where to Start

The R/C recipe
for getting under way

YOU HAVE ACCEPTED the fact that, as a home economist, you must communicate ideas. You know that you will do this in photographs and art, in written and spoken words. You realize the importance of getting home-centered ideas across effectively. But the question is and always has been, *where and how does one start*?

How does one get under way in writing a recipe release for a newspaper foods page? Planning a demonstration of pie-making for a group of homemakers or students? Setting up a table of foods to be photographed? Preparing slides that show certain techniques in sewing? Figuring a fresh way to put across the principles of good nutrition or good family relations? Or following through on any of the other tasks that come under the broad term, Home Economics Communications?

There is no such thing as "instant writing." Every piece of worth-reading copy must be planned and replanned, organized and reorganized, written and rewritten, checked and rechecked, if it is to measure up to the standards of accuracy,

*Writing is like cooking; it's
easier when you have a recipe to
follow. For the R/C "Recipe," see page 8.*

brevity, clarity, and visibility. You will find, however, that the fundamentals of Home Economics Communications are simple. They boil down into this easy-to-remember recipe:

THE R/C* RECIPE FOR EFFECTIVE COMMUNICATIONS

Step 1. *Visualize* your audience. Visualize also the space and the format in which your material is to appear.

Step 2. *Analyze* your problems. Figure out how to solve them, or to work around them.

Step 3. *Organize* your thinking. Study out the order in which your points should be presented.

Step 4. *Dramatize* your presentation. But do it in a way that is appropriate and timely.

Step 5. *Synchronize* all of these. Then synchronize your ideas with the ideas of others.

VISUALIZE Your Audience

Ask any successful editor, writer, or public speaker. He will tell you that the big thing in writing or speaking is to "get through" to his audience. He will say that the way to do this is to think of any audience — listening or reading — not as a huge group, but as individuals, with individual problems, aims, and desires. In other words, visualize people — as persons!

Let's face it. Home economics information invariably suggests work-to-be-done. Few women

Be a Question-Asker

You can scarcely hope to visualize and understand homemakers unless you talk with them. Asking some simple question, as "How do you like your new dryer?" can get a conversation rolling; help you to build background; help you to be a more understanding writer.

---

*Richardson-Callahan. The original R/C formula consisted of only the first four of these steps — Visualize, Analyze, Organize, Dramatize. The fifth step, "Synchronize," has been added to make the formula more applicable to new problems in communications.

or girls will deliberately read or listen to a discussion of work, except as each sees in it something that benefits herself or her family, directly or indirectly. Your first job is to examine your ideas and information to make sure they are both sound and suitable for the group; then tempt (if not decoy) your audience into wanting to learn what you have to say. To do this you must have a mental picture of typical members of that audience firmly in your mind.

To visualize an audience of today's homemakers is not easy. When Home Economics was very young, Mrs. Homemaker was, in general, a woman who stayed at home, looked after her family, did her own cooking and sewing, and rather frowned on those who did not follow this accepted pattern. Today's homemaker may be any one of many types.

She may be a career wife who hires a part-time housekeeper to look after the children. She may be a young — or older — business girl, living alone in a studio apartment. She may be a woman-on-the-go who depends entirely on housekeeping shortcuts and convenience foods. She may be a very young mother with little money. She may be a Senior Citizen doing lonely cooking and having little interest in it. She may live in a city flat or in a suburban split-level; in a tract house or a trailer.

But one thing is certain. All real homemakers have one thing in common — a desire to benefit their families and/or themselves.

Having satisfied yourself, then, that your idea offers some genuine benefit to a good proportion of those diverse homemakers, you can forget that you are writing to great numbers of them. Instead, mentally visualize some one person and write directly to her. Surprisingly, when you do this, many another homemaker will feel that you are writing especially to and for her.

REMEMBER . . .

"In writing, be positive— not negative. Think in terms of readers rather than subject matter. Think in terms of tomorrow — not of yesterday. Build your castles high in the air, then put foundations under them."

"Understand the facts. If you don't understand them, neither will the reader. Don't show off. Don't pose as knowing more than you really do."

"Writers must do all of the work; readers none. Do not write down to readers, do not write up to them; write alongside of them."

"Strive for phrase-making. But don't overdo it. A punch line in every sentence leaves readers groggy."

"Tact means to be in touch with people; to be able to foresee the effect our words and actions will have upon them."

VISUALIZE Copy In Its Finished Format

There is more to visualizing than just picturing the individuals who make up your audience. You need a mental picture, too, of how your copy is going to look in its finished form. When you go about preparing a booklet, think of it — see it! — as an actual booklet, not as just so many recipes or typewritten pages. When you write a recipe for a label on a can or carton, think of how your copy will look in type in that too-tiny block of space. This ability to "see" what you are writing translated into type and layout is one of the big secrets in writing. When you learn to do this, you will find it infinitely easier to write copy that fits the space allowed for it.

ANALYZE Your Problems

Whatever the task to be done, there are always problems, always limitations. Certainly this is true of those on-the-job planning and writing tasks that confront most home economists.

Your problem of the moment may be limitation of space (too small a booklet to cover the subject matter adequately); limitation of time (not enough of it — you think! — to present your lesson plans); limitation of budget (not enough money for color photographs or top-quality art work). Whatever the problems, accept them, then work around them with an objective, uncomplaining point of view.

If you learn that the involved recipe you want to use must be shortened to six lines, shorten it. (Better yet, discard it and substitute a short recipe.) If there is no budget for photography or art, break up the pages with interesting type arrangements — subheads, occasional variations in styles and sizes of type, and the like. If you must give a cooking school without an assistant, get the

EYE WITNESS

To be a writer you need three eyes. Use your two natural ones to observe all that goes on around you, and your third or mind's eye to visualize what you are writing. The more you develop that third eye, the better able you will be to write in your mind — to work out articles or ideas mentally before you take pencil in hand.

audience into the act. There is always a way to work out any problem. And the result usually turns out to be fresher and more interesting because you have been forced to take a new approach.

Certainly there is not enough time on any job to waste any of it in complaining about obstacles. Strong home economics writing is done with a positive pen, never a negative one!

ORGANIZE Your Thinking

What makes one piece of copy easy to read and a joy to follow, while other copy is hazy and confusing? The answer lies in how clearly the writer thinks, and how hard she is willing to work to organize her thoughts. It's as simple as that. For without clear thinking and logical organization, writing is inclined to be tentative and "little-girlish," rather than positive and professional.

And where do you start in that thinking and organizing? First, figure out the big idea that you want to put across. You are writing, let's say, about the new way to clean an oven. The big thought you want to put across is that oven-cleaning is easy when your method is used. Keep that thought uppermost in your mind.

Next, line up your facts and decide the order in which they should be presented. Decide on your point of view. Will you write in the first person (that is, say, in effect, "This is how I do it")? Or will you write in the second person, saying, "Do this, do that"? Or in the third person, impersonal, saying that ovens can be cleaned by doing this or that? Make sure you keep the same point of view throughout your story.

Sort out your best attention-catcher. Use it as a lead to get your story off to a quick start. Then write what you have to say in logical sequence, using simple words, sentences of varying length, and no over-long paragraphs.

CLEAR WRITING

Clear writing is the direct result of clear thinking. Until you learn to think, you cannot possibly produce clear, easy-to-follow copy.

MORE ABOUT POINT OF VIEW

In all writing, establish a specific point of view and keep to it. If you find it advisable to switch point of view, make it obvious that you are doing so intentionally. If, for example, you wish to interpolate a bit of personal experience in a signed article written in the second person, set the interpolation apart by means of dashes or parentheses.

Try following this pattern. See if your copy doesn't march along as all good copy should.

Yes, it takes self-discipline to work with scattered thoughts until you have them under control. But such self-imposed discipline is the girdle that gives shape and form to ideas. Without such a girdle your writing will be shapeless, bulging with adjectives and loose sentences. And it will rarely be followed with any degree of interest!

IT'S A FACT

In all forms of communications, there is no substitute for simple clarity.

DRAMATIZE Your Presentation

Every piece of copy, every program plan, every type of home economics communications needs to be dramatized. This doesn't mean fancy writing, or superficial acting, or over-dressed photographic settings. The true meaning of the word "dramatize" is to "bring to life." And dramatization is most effective when done simply.

Take your cue from the successful playwright. One reason he turns out truly dramatic productions is because he understands people. He knows how they respond to various emotions, how they react under certain circumstances. He creates an atmosphere by establishing a mood — through costumes and stage settings as well as through the actors' lines. Most of all he is able to achieve drama because he actually "lives" his characters as he writes about them.

DRAMATIC THOUGHT

Whatever you use in a decorative way, give it importance! That rule — preached and practiced by all designers — applies equally in dramatizing ideas. Make important facts stand out importantly. When you do, your copy will stand up and stand out.

Photographs, art work, charts, and other visuals all help to put life into home-centered facts. So do lively pictorial words and expressions. But most of all, dramatization starts with being alive yourself, full of enthusiasm for what you are doing and for the people you are hoping to interest. It is never enough merely to spark an idea. You must make it sparkle all the way. That means you must keep a sparkle in yourself, as well as in what you write or say.

SYNCHRONIZE Everything!

When you have mentally visualized, analyzed, organized, and dramatized your material, you have the ingredients assembled for a clear-cut presentation of the idea. But as in any good recipe, those ingredients must be blended together. In other words, *synchronized*. Although the original interpretation of "synchronize" had to do with timing, the word now also means a merging or meshing together of various elements. That is the meaning here.

One way to explain the term and to tie it into the other parts of the writing formula is with this simple visual. (The "spoon" blends together the four "basic ingredients!")

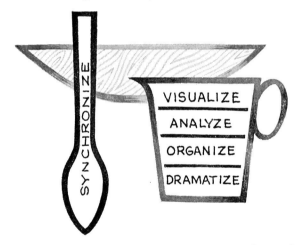

PARAGRAPHS

Changes in length of paragraphs make a piece of copy easy to read. For variety, some should be short, some long.

SENTENCES

In providing a change of pace, s e n t e n c e s also should vary in length. A good *average* is about 17 words. Sentences in books can be somewhat longer than those used in newspapers.

VERBS

One of the best ways to spark up copy is to use plenty of action verbs. Study the sports section of a newspaper. See how the verbs pop out; how they make the copy move.

There is more to synchronization than this blending. It is equally important to synchronize your ideas with the ideas of your associates.

For whatever you do in home economics — teaching, business, research, or whatever — you do not work alone. There are always others to be considered. In business, the promotion department, sales department, production department,

Most fiction writers work harder than do most factual writers. When the factual writer, like the fiction writer, puts all of her creative ability and writing skill into a piece of copy, factual writing hits a new high.

One famous foods writer says, "Keep a notebook. In it jot down interesting notes about things you see and hear and eat; themes in store windows; menus; table decorations — all such things. You'll find these unorganized scribbles frequently provide an idea when one is needed."

the art director, the photographer, the salesman, and, yes, the other home economists in the organization will have an interest in your plans. If you are a teacher, your program will be influenced by the superintendent, principal, students, parents, curriculum restrictions, and community reactions. Every magazine has a publisher, editor-in-chief, department editors, art directors, rewrite editors, and copy readers — all with ideas as definite as your own. Any phase of government work involves countless agencies making a chain of regulations and recommendations that reach from the seat of government to the top of your own desk. And in every organization (including home economics groups) there are dozens or hundreds of persons, all with strong ideas and convictions.

The important thing to remember is that in this age of interdependence and teamwork, greater goals are achieved when you synchronize (that is, merge) your thinking with that of others concerned with the same basic problems. Never let yourself be an *island*. Be a *peninsula*, projecting your ideas and ingenuity without detaching them from the mainland thinking of others with whom you work.

Visualize, Analyze, Organize, Dramatize, Synchronize — the R/C Recipe for communicating ideas effectively. In the pages that follow, this recipe will be expanded, restated, and fitted to cover the various subjects that will help you communicate ideas.

Authors' Note: Since lists of reference books and supplementary aids have a way of going out of date quickly, we have omitted such material from this revised edition of "How to Write for Homemakers." Our reasoning is that most of you who will read and use this book are thoughtful readers of the Journal of Home Economics and other professional home economics magazines. Through the editorial and advertising columns of such publications you are kept informed as to the latest in worthwhile books, booklets, filmstrips, and other teaching aids. We urge you to follow them closely.

3.

Photography and Art Work

How to produce good pictures

How to use pictures effectively

EVERY HOME ECONOMIST today is concerned with pictures.

Business home economists are called on to plan and set up photographs or to supply ideas for art work for a variety of uses: labels and hang-tags; booklets and leaflets; articles and releases; filmstrips and posters; store displays and television commercials. Home economists in extension service find it necessary to plan and often produce illustrations for bulletins and circulars and other uses.

Home economists in various fields — television, teaching, business, extension, and the like — find pictures an ever-present aid in explaining and dramatizing important homemaking information and techniques.

This chapter, then, begins with the planning and production of photographs for specific uses, then proceeds with suggestions for using photographs and art to best advantage.

Pictures are windows in walls of words. With them it is possible to open up new vistas for homemakers.

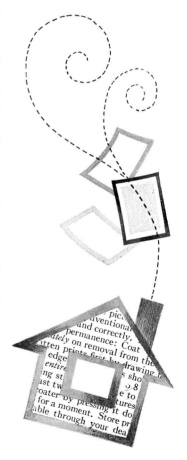

When Your Job Is To Produce Photographs

Working as you do — or will — in a picture-minded world, your job (especially if you are a home economist in business) is almost certain to include setting up photographs. Whether you are new in the field or an experienced "pro," you soon find that every one of those photographs poses not one but several problems. Question is: How do you tackle them? Where and how do you start in planning a photograph?

Let's go back to the R/C Recipe for Effective Communications, and see how it applies here.

STEP 1. ANALYZE THE PROBLEM

Whether you are to photograph a cake or a casserole, a coat for a child, or a corner of a kitchen, start by asking yourself, *"What do I want this picture to say? What important idea do I want to put across?"* Remember, there must be a basic reason behind every picture. Unless you can figure out what that reason is, there's no point in your doing the photograph!

Let's consider food photos first, for two reasons: (1) There are many more home economists involved in photographing food than in getting pictures of fashions, home equipment, room arrangements, or other subjects. (2) The points brought out about planning and setting up food arrangements apply basically to the photographing of other subjects. Special notes about special problems will be found in the marginal notes that appear in this chapter.

You're to photograph a cake, for example. First, determine your basic idea. Do you want to say, "Look at the texture of this cake — isn't it perfect?" Or, "See this brand new idea for a birthday cake." Or, "This is an easy way to cover that frosting with chopped walnuts."

COLOR NOTE

Black-and-white photography is not really black and white. It is gray against gray! Visualize each item as it will appear without color — in light or dark or medium gray. A simple rule is to put dark-colored objects on lighter background, and vice versa. Beware, however, of too sharp contrast.

DETAILS SHOW UP

Every detail counts in photography. If there are wrinkles in the background material, or if the paint is peeling, those defects will be apparent in the finished picture.

Once you have settled that all-important question, you are ready to approach other problems that enter into the planning. Your thinking may run something like this: If that cake is to show texture, the problem will be how best to show the cut cake or a slice of it. If it is to suggest a new idea for a birthday cake, the problem will be not only to think up the new idea, but to get some birthday excitement into the picture. If the aim is to show using chopped walnuts on the cake, it may need to be an action shot. If the cake photograph is to go on a package of cake mix, it must say, "Wonderful cake," and nothing else. For a magazine advertisement, it must tell the product story at a glance.

Reasoning out those problems in advance helps one define the job, which in turn makes the job itself much easier.

STEP 2. VISUALIZE YOUR PHOTOGRAPH IN FINISHED FORM

Early in your planning, get a mental image of how that photograph is going to look when it's finished. Is it to be in color or black-and-white? Will it occupy a full page in a good-sized booklet, or be reduced to small space in a leaflet? Will it be reproduced on smooth paper stock or on newsprint? Do you see it as a vertical shot or a horizontal one?

As the planning progresses you may change your concept a number of times, or have it changed for you. Even so, it is good to "see" that preliminary picture in your mind's eye. By doing so the photograph becomes a reality, and you see ways to improve it with strong additions and fresh ideas. But you will also see new problems popping up!

If the picture is to be a black-and-white, one problem will be to determine what colors to use

BEWARE!

Avoid putting dark accessories at the back of a food photograph. Dark objects tend to draw the eyes back, rather than to focus them on the center of interest. Frequently the faint shadow of a leaf is more effective than the dark leaf itself.

WHAT SIZE?

Glossy prints 5" x 7" or 8" x 10" are best for publicity purposes ... When sending a photo of a person or persons, be sure to supply complete name or names. If you are asked for a photograph of yourself to be used in publicity, never be guilty of sending a glamour one.

in backgrounds, dishes, and foods. If it is to be a full page in color, as in a magazine, you'll probably need more items or a more dramatic composition than if the photograph were to be in black-and-white and reduced to small space. (The marginal notes that appear here, together with the chapter, "Food Photogenics," suggest a number of problems that often face home economists together with possible solutions.)

POSTERS

Every poster should present a central idea, and be readable across a classroom—about 30 feet.

The important thing is to have an advance mental image of the finished photograph, and then work around the problems of details as they arise.

STEP 3. FIGURE WAYS TO DRAMATIZE

Next step in working on a photographic plan is to figure out what you can do to lift the photo out of the ordinary and inject excitement into it. That is, dramatize it. Getting in this dramatic impact is largely the responsibility of the home economist working together with photographer and art director.

How do you make a photograph dramatic? This is an often asked question that may be answered in any or all of these ways:

By conceiving a fresh new idea or getting a new twist into an old one . . . By selecting props and accessories (if that is your responsibility) which heighten style and appetite appeal . . . By using sizable objects for the major points of interest. And always, always, by seeing to it that every picture has one — and only one — center of interest!

ABOUT BACKGROUNDS

Background in a photograph must be exactly that. It should never be more obvious or obtrusive than the item being photographed.

As a home economist-stylist, you must step up the importance, the "flair," of whatever is important to the picture. In a food picture, this means giving height to flatness, shape to the shapeless, color to the colorless, as discussed in the chapter, "Food Photogenics." (See page 177.)

FOOD CLOSE-UPS USED EDITORIALLY

This is an example of the realistic type of food photograph which many home economists must prepare for use editorially in booklets, books, filmstrips, and magazines. For such use, a photograph — whether in color or not — serves several purposes. Almost always it attracts attention to and "sells" a recipe, rather than a specific food product. Often, as here, it plays up some interesting serving idea. Sometimes, as here, it suggests other food items that might complete the menu. *Suggestion:* Turn now to page 24 and compare the treatment of the casserole in that advertising photo with this editorial one.

Photograph courtesy of Better Homes and Gardens.

PROBLEMS IN ROOM PHOTOGRAPHY

According to photographers who specialize in architectural details, every room photograph should show something of the ceiling and the floor, in addition to wall area, without over-emphasizing the floor. In both these pictures, blank floor space has been minimized by placing furniture down in the foreground.

Photographs courtesy of Better Homes and Gardens.

DETAILS

Note how the rusty-red of the chairs gives color depth to the photograph above. Without it, the various tints, textures and details would tend to fall apart in so complicated a composition. Photo at right was simpler to compose because there are fewer elements. Observe how the figures in each photograph help to bring the scene to life; give it mobility. See, too, how the suspended lights help to break up wall areas while adding a special note of interest.

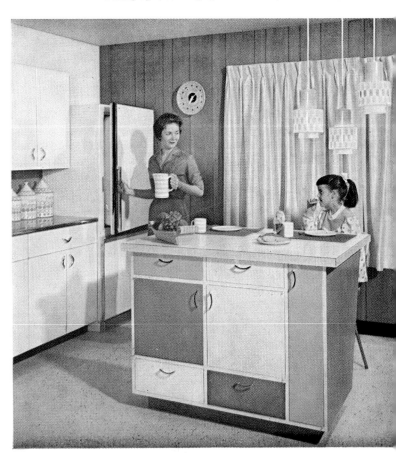

IMPORTANCE OF ANGLE

In photographing a piece of furniture or equipment, the angle from which the picture is taken is important. Here the photographer has shot across one corner of the custom-built sink to bring the center of interest down into the right-hand corner of picture. By so doing he has (1) played up the piece of equipment; (2) taken full advantage of the colorful paneled wall beyond; (3) succeeded in breaking up the expanse of floor. With it all he has managed to give the impression that there is more to the kitchen than meets the eye.

Photograph courtesy of Better Homes and Gardens.

PRODUCT PROMOTION. This is a black and white reproduction of a four-color photograph used in the booklet, "Glamour Ways With Cottage Cheese." The idea: serving cottage cheese for breakfast — hence the breakfast table setup. Tablecloth was a sunny yellow; napkin, sky blue. Cup and saucer were a deeper gray-blue, matching the blue of the white-rimmed plate. Note how these shades come through in tones of gray; note the sparkle of white.

Photograph courtesy of Dairy Council of California. Elmer Moss, Photographer.

PRODUCT PUBLICITY. Aim of the home economist in this photograph was to suggest a new and natural use for a whipped cream topping — one that would play up the product to good advantage. Since the photo was to be part of a summer promotion, the answer was a cool coffee gelatin designed to double as dessert and *demitasse*, with hand demonstrating the product in use. Note how thumb is placed to obscure the brand name on can.

Photograph courtesy of Avoset Company, makers of Qwip dessert topping. Elmer Moss, Photographer.

[23]

FOOD CLOSE-UPS IN ADVERTISING

A photograph used to illustrate a recipe in a food advertisement must display the product to best advantage. That can be difficult when the food is difficult to recognize in cooked form. Here the product is cream style corn; the recipe, a Frankfurter Corn Bake. Note those tiny kernels brought up so carefully to the surface before baking. Frankfurter slices, catsup, and parsley break up the broad surface. Simple white dishes call attention to color and texture of food.

Photograph courtesy California Packing Corporation — Del Monte Brand Foods.

[24]

PHOTOGRAPHING FOOD OUT OF DOORS

When subject matter fits logically into the situation, and when weather conditions are favorable, interesting results can be obtained in photographing foods out of doors. So many factors enter in that much experimentation can be done. This photograph was shot in direct sunlight against the blue of a lake in Golden Gate Park, San Francisco. Photographers of this picture, and of the one opposite as well, were Frank and Dorothy Williams.

Photograph courtesy California Packing Corporation -- Del Monte Brand Foods.

PHOTOGRAPH OF AN IDEA

Here a recipe-idea has been reduced to a practically self-explanatory photo plus simple yet clear directions. "Don't even take the slices out of the can," says the caption. "Just pour off liquid and replace with lime gelatin (made with **half** the water in package directions). Chill until set. Run a little **hot** water on can sides and bottom to loosen. Then cut bottom from can and use to punch mold out." To emphasize the product still further, there's the pineapple-shaped platter in an Hawaiian setting.

Photograph courtesy of Dole Corporation.

STEP 4. ORGANIZE YOUR PLAN OF WORK

Once your photograph is firmed in your mind, you are ready to organize your plan of work, starting, probably, with props and accessories. Next (if it is to be a food photograph) comes trying out the chosen recipe to fit the props, and marketing for the picture. In doing this organizing, keep in mind this fact: Regardless of how exactly you may plan, the picture may undergo changes under the camera. Be prepared for everything.

This means taking not one cake or pie or loaf of nut bread to the studio, but three or four of them. Something may go wrong in the cutting, or the art director or photographer may decide on a new approach. Make sure you have a liberal assortment of background materials; a variety of plates in different sizes and shapes and/or cake stands of varying heights. For a salad photograph never stop with one or two heads of lettuce, but take several of several varieties so the photographer can select just the type and tone of leaf that is needed. If you're using flowers, take along a number of kinds and colors. (In general, flowers of sharp design and sparse foliage work better than small flowers with heavy foliage. That is why marguerites appear so often in pictures.)

It is a strange sight to see the home economist on her way to the studio with car or taxicab filled to capacity with bags and bundles, baskets and boxes. But if, along with her load, she carries a generous amount of patience and enthusiasm, the photographing day is likely to go smoothly.

STEP 5. SYNCHRONIZE YOUR IDEAS WITH THOSE OF OTHERS

When you are working "on your own" with a photographer to produce a picture, you have one set of responsibilities, he another. The more you

WHEN YOU SHOP FOR PROPS

Consider how the photograph is to be used. If it is to reach readers of newspapers or general magazines, select dishes and silver and utensils of general appeal and availability. In a magazine that stresses new ideas, look for new items. . . In a booklet or a book, keep to the conservative.

Beware of bold patterns in dishes — they compete with food. Same is true of bold wallpapers in a how-to-do-it furniture arrangement.

synchronize your thinking with his, the better the results.

Your job is to explain to the photographer just what idea you want to put across. Show him what is to go into the picture, as you see it. Set out the props to discuss with him. Consult with him as to the degree of brownness for the roast, the height of the cake, the choice of the servers. Let him set up the picture as he visualizes it, rather than insist on composing it yourself. Then study that preliminary composition through the ground glass of the camera. If you have a recommendation for improving the arrangement or lighting, offer it, and give reasons why. But keep an open-minded point of view. Remember, a good photograph is not an accident. It is a work of art on which you and the photographer collaborate. The more smoothly you work together, the better the finished picture.

Suppose a home economist is working in an area where no good commercial photographer is available. Should she try to take photographs herself?

Rarely. If she is a far-better-than-usual amateur photographer, and if in her work she needs slides or black-and-white pictures of rooms or furniture arrangements or the like to show on a screen, she may find it advantageous to do some on her own. (See marginal notes on photographing rooms.)

Should she try to photograph food setups? Probably not, except experimentally as a hobby, or as a pictorial record of her work. Good food photography is highly complicated, requiring specialized and expensive equipment and endless care and patience with details — plus years of training on the part of the photographer.

The home economist working alone (or with an inexperienced photographer) is almost sure to find difficulty with several factors: Unless a setup is lighted just right, from sides and back as well as

SHOW-HOW AND ACTION SHOTS

In posing hand pictures, plan to have the hand, or hands, serve as arrow or arrows directing attention to the most important item or operation.

In a how-to-do-it photograph, keep to one operation or idea. Avoid trying to get across too much in any one picture.

STYLE NOTE

Since skirt lengths date a photograph or drawing, it's a good idea to avoid them whenever possible. Same is true of exaggerated hairdos and fads in accessories.

front, dark shadows show up where they are not wanted, and objects flatten out, losing all their "modeling" — their three-dimensional quality. Unless the camera is focused properly, vertical lines (such as candles, water glasses, and other tall objects) come out far from vertical in the picture. Unless the camera angle is just right, strange things happen to a lovingly planned composition.

What is the answer if you are faced with that unusual problem? Take a course in photography. Then find an eager-to-cooperate photographer and work with him until, together, you produce the kind of pictures that are demanded in a highly competitive picture world.

Notes on Using Photographs and Photographic Reproductions

Whenever a photograph is used to highlight a point (as in a speech or platform demonstration or in the classroom) it should, if possible, be projected onto a screen so that all can see and study it. It is distracting to pass pictures from student to student in a lesson period. It is disconcerting when a lecturer holds up a picture that is not clearly visible from the back of the room. It is annoying when a televised photograph is held at an angle that obscures the principal point of the picture.

In selecting photographs for screen projection (including television screens), be truly selective. Make sure that every picture gets across just one pertinent point; leave the picture on the screen long enough to transfer that point to the minds of the viewers. This means that every photograph so used should (1) be simply composed with no unnecessary frills or accessories; (2) have no distracting background, no accessories that might focus the attention on them, rather than on the idea; and (3) be free from shadows that look like holes when enlarged on the screen.

SEWING TECHNIQUES

To photograph a point in cutting, use small-figured material on a plain cutting surface. This makes the idea come through well.

To show stitching, use heavier-than-usual thread, larger-than-usual stitches. If sensible, show the stitches on plain cloth rather than on figured.

Use as little background as possible. Put all the emphasis on the point you wish to get across.

ROOM PHOTOGRAPHY

Avoid straight-on shots. Work from an angle.

Avoid big expanses of bare floor or walls.

Suggest that there's more to the room than shows. This can be done by getting in just part of a chair or table.

Let there be a fire in the fireplace. Otherwise it will look empty. A newspaper, lighted just before the shooting, will give a quick blaze.

Look out for pictures on walls. Study them carefully in the camera. Think twice before you show a mirror!

Pictures and other visuals used on bulletin boards and in static displays call for ingenuity and fresh thinking on the part of the teacher.

Familiar examples: Running a string from a point of interest in the picture into the margin where the point is explained. Tacking up pictures that show how to serve or eat unusual foods — *artichokes*, for instance. Featuring a menu from a gourmet restaurant, and, at the sides, translating what the French terms mean — *ragout of lamb*, for example.

Unusual example: The home economics teacher who, upon learning that Johnny Somebody was the top-of-the-juke box singer of the moment, wrote to said Johnny (in care of a television station that had featured him as a guest star). In her letter she asked if he would have his publicity studio do a photograph of himself eating a substantial breakfast, complete with glass of milk. Johnny followed through, sent the photograph with a personal autograph to the girls at Horace Mann High. Needless to say, it was the bulletin board high-spot of the year!

What About Art Work?

Instead of photographs, you or the art director or some other executive may decide to use drawings. Now your problem becomes a slightly different one.

In planning a photograph you are dealing with known quantities. You know that the cake you set before the camera will come out much as you see it there — though it may not look as high as it really is. In picturing a cake in a drawing, however, you are dealing with unknown quantities. The artist is certain to inject some of his own personality into the finished art. The art director is sure to project his ideas. Here, again, the thing to do is to synchronize your thinking with that of others concerned.

In working directly with any commercial artist, these recommendations usually obtain good results.

1. Take time to define the job to him or her. Think twice, however, before you say flatly, "This is what I want done." Instead give the artist a mental picture of the problems involved, and see what he may evolve from them.

2. Show him the amount of copy that must be used. If feasible, give him a carbon of what you have written.

3. Figure out in advance whether there is some special technique which may be difficult for him to understand, some utensil or piece of equipment with which he is not familiar. If so, be prepared with "scrap" (i.e., clippings of illustrations) that show such details. If no scrap is to be found, you may need to make up a cake for him to study, or pose your own hands to show him how the homemaker would naturally hold the spoon or pour the batter.

4. Send him to his studio with a feeling of enthusiasm for the job and an understanding of what is to be done. Make him know that you have confidence in him.

5. But always, always, ask him to bring in a penciled rough of the sketches before he puts them into final form. He will not object to making necessary changes on the roughs. But, like all of us, he is disturbed at doing finished things over.

6. Remember that the artist, like you, wants to be proud of the finished job. Cooperate with him to bring that about.

As stated in Chapter 1, pictures play a big part in modern communications. The big thing to remember is that every picture must have one center of interest. That center of interest corresponds to the topic sentence in a piece of writing. In the next chapter that matter of the topic sentence will be discussed in detail.

TO ATTACH A CAPTION

When a photograph goes out with manuscript or release, include a caption for it. If the caption is long, type it on letter-size paper and key it to the photo by numbers or letters. If it is only a few lines long, type it on a half-sheet and attach it to the lower edge of photo with rubber cement or gummed tape.

Photographs for editorial or school use should be free from brand names.

MAILING PHOTOGRAPHS

Be extremely careful in mailing photos. Use plenty of stiff cardboard. Mark the envelope, "PHOTOS. DO NOT BEND." Never use paper clips on photographs or on manuscript enclosed with photographs. Never write on the back of a photograph with hard pencil or ballpoint pen. If you must write at all, use wax crayon or soft pencil, and don't bear down.

Magazine readership surveys show that the lower left hand quarter of a full-page food photograph is a highly important spot. Hence is is a good place for some highly important item.

THE PICTURE AHEAD

One important thing to keep in mind is that in both art and photography, techniques are constantly changing, and that you, the home economist, must change with them. This can be interesting because it permits you to share in the creating of a new approach. At the same time it presents you with additional problems and responsibilities.

Take the current experiments in photographing foods out of doors, for example. Whether it is done for the sake of an unusual setting (as suggested in the photograph on page 25) or to provide a specific lighting effect, you may face all sorts of minor difficulties, such as having the wind blow the lettuce off the salad or bees buzz the flowers! But these are relatively unimportant. In every photograph your big job is to make certain that the food idea itself is both interesting and practical from the homemakers' point of view.

IT'S YOUR TURN

Authors' Note: Turn back to the color plates of food advertising on pages 24, 25, and 26. With the permission of the companies concerned, each of these has been cut down to fit the page size of this book. Such "cropping" is, in itself, an art and one that the home economist will do well to study. You may like to turn now, too, to Chapter 21, "Food Photogenics," page 177. You'll note it is a "working" chapter, with items arranged alphabetically for easy reference when a problem in arranging some food for photographing comes up.

4.

The Topic Sentence

How to stitch scattered thoughts into a basic idea

MANY TIMES when writing or speaking, you'll be directed to "keep your copy short," or to "boil down what you have to say."

At first this may seem difficult if not impossible to do. It becomes easier when you learn to apply this fundamental rule:

In all communications — written or spoken — narrow down your thoughts to the one principal idea you want to put across, then expand that idea to fit within the limitations of time or space. Until you do this, you are not ready to write or speak at any length.

Whether you are planning a demonstration, writing an article for a magazine, or preparing a speech or a program, keep asking yourself, "What am I trying to say? What is my message?" Keep nagging at it until you distill your thinking into a single statement. There is your topic sentence.

In a sustained piece of writing, as in a book, that distilled thought is called the Central Theme. Every worth-reading book has one.

The topic sentence is the thread that gathers thoughts together and stitches them into a central idea.

Bruce Catton, author of a number of books about the Civil War, once said, "I write about the GI — the ordinary foot soldier of that war." There, in a sentence, is the central theme that runs through his books.

In this book, "How to Write for Homemakers," the central theme is suggested in the first chapter: *Be sure that everything you write creates pictures in the minds of homemakers. Be sure that every photograph you set up — or use — says something interesting or worthwhile.* To support that theme, the other 20 chapters of the book set forth suggestions designed to help young home economists in specific writing and photographic jobs that go with home economics communications.

Applying the Principle

How does the topic-sentence-central-theme principle apply to types of home economics communications other than writing? Let's look at five home economists.

A sewing teacher declared: "If I don't do another thing this term, I'm going to teach those youngsters how to use pins in sewing." Of course she taught much more than pinning, but all of her teaching was strengthened because she had pinpointed her aim.

One dietitian planning a school lunch program said, "If through my way of writing quantity recipes I can just help the cafeteria cooks to develop judgment in their cooking, we'll have good food." She knew what was needed. She knew what she wanted to do. And she did it!

A home economist working for a utility company decided to do a demonstration featuring small pieces of equipment. In narrowing down her thinking she said, "I might show how to prepare a meal without turning on the range." Narrowing still further she decided to demonstrate how a hostess, using electric skillet, blender, toaster, coffeemaker, and the like, could prepare supper in the living room without leaving the scene of the party even temporarily. This she did, calling her demonstration, "How to Be a Guest at Your Own Party." Needless to say a good time was had by everyone in the audience.

One homemaker, finding that the training of her children was going in all directions, took a day to herself to ponder the question, "What is the one big thing I want to instill in my children?" Her pondering led her to decide that, above all else, she wanted to teach her children not only to think for themselves, but to think about others. With this for her main objective, small details in behavior took on proper perspective.

One business home economist, looking at a food setup ready to be photographed, said, "There's something wrong here. There is no one center of interest." She then proceeded to rearrange the foods, eliminating some of the dishes, pushing others into the background.

See how it works? Once you can put a handle on your idea, you can carry it any distance.

In advertising, that distilled thought (i.e., topic sentence) forms the headline. In a magazine article it is usually the title or the lead paragraph. In a demonstration, speech, or program, the name or theme (in other words, the topic sentence) constitutes the "bait" which tempts people to come and hear what will be said.

Let us assume, then, that you have distilled your thinking into a principal idea. You are now ready to expand and develop it in more detail.

How do you do this? With paragraphs.

AVOID GENERALITIES

For color, variety, vigor, and clarity, be specific. In a market release, for example, avoid general statements as, "Now is the time to make jams and jellies." Instead, say (in effect), "Make strawberry jam this week (or month) while berries are at their cheapest and best."

THEME

The theme of a piece of writing should appear in the lead and be kept running like a thread throughout — though not to the point of being tiresome or obvious.

Paragraphs Are Important

"All writing," says one teacher, "begins with the lowly paragraph." She then goes on to say, "If you can write a well-constructed paragraph, you can write a library."

What constitutes a well-constructed paragraph? Much depends on its containing one sentence that is all-important. In other words, every paragraph needs a "mother sentence" that is stronger than the other sentences which might be thought of as "children."

One way to test the strength of your own paragraph structures is to reread something you have written. Then, with pencil in hand, underscore the principal sentence in each paragraph. Whether it appears at the beginning of the paragraph, in the middle, or at the end is not important, just so it is there. But if those "mother sentences" are lacking, the "children sentences" are almost certain to get out of hand!

(*Possible exception:* In recipes and directions, sentences are usually of equal value. No one sentence dominates a paragraph.)

Once you learn the value of the central theme, the topic sentence, you will find your writing strengthened. You will be less likely to switch from one point of view to another in the same paragraph. You will not be tempted to string sentences together with those measly little words, "and" and "but." Because you have weighed your thoughts, you will substitute definitive words for empty ones.

Good writing is a mass of complexities. It is made up of themes within themes; strong paragraphs growing out of the main topic sentence of a piece of writing. Yet all writing is reducible to fundamentals. The better you understand those fundamentals, the simpler the complexities become.

Now, we (R/C) ask ourselves: What one basic idea did we hope to get across in this chapter? Just this: Narrow down your thinking to a single topic sentence, then expand it within the limits of time or space. Look upon it as the sturdy thread that can "stitch up" a piece of writing or an oral presentation, and make it hold together!

FATHER KNOWS BEST

A criticism often made of home economics writing is that it sounds "girlish." Perhaps the criticism is sound, perhaps not. But whether or not, it's well to get a man's comment on what you write. His direct way of stating facts will help you to put strength into your copy.

QUOTABLES FROM NOTABLES

Why is Mark Twain widely quoted? Because he had the ability to short-cut a thought in a fresh, sharp way that made it memorable. Why do we remember lines from the poems of Emily Dickinson? For the same reason. You can apply the same technique when writing about home things.

5.

Directions

How to make them
measure up to standard

WHATEVER LINE OF WORK you follow in the field of home economics, you are certain to have to write directions. The need for good writing of directions increases daily, as new home products, new home appliances and equipment, and new ways of doing familiar homemaking tasks are developed.

Generally speaking, there are three types of directions needed by homemakers. (1) Directions for *using* something. (2) Directions for *making* something. (3) Directions for *doing* something. (Recipe writing, of course, may involve any or all of these three types of directions. Since it is so highly specialized, the subject will be discussed separately and in detail in the next chapter.)

Directions for Writing Directions

1. *Make sure you really understand the process or the operation you are undertaking to explain.* That means you must get personally acquainted with the product or tool or method — get the feel

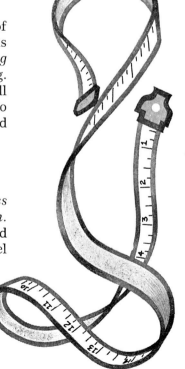

Directions, like a tape measure, must be accurate, easy to use, and exactly the right length.

of it — before you attempt to write. Discover possible problems that the homemaker may meet, and figure how to keep her from being baffled and irritated by them. (Haven't you personally felt completely frustrated by a new type of can opener or "easy-opening" carton, or some other complicated device?) No woman likes to feel that a piece of equipment is smarter than she is!

2. *Think the process through.* Act it out as you are thinking. What do you do first? Second? Third? Write down each step in that order, beginning each step with the verb that best expresses the meaning. By starting each step with a verb, you will find it easier to keep your directions in good order and make them march along quickly.

SHORTEN TO STRENGTHEN

After you have written any set of directions, go through what you have written and take out every unnecessary word — especially those empty words such as "a," "an," and "the." Note how this strengthens your copy, helps it to march along.

3. *Think about the space those directions will occupy.* Will they have to be squeezed down to fit a small hang-tag for a blouse, a panel on a carton or bottle of detergent, a few lines on a package of frozen fish? Or are they to be handled in larger type and more words in a folder or leaflet accompanying that new vacuum cleaner? Or may they be expanded into a bulletin or booklet of complete instructions for making slip covers or removing stains? (If it's to be the last-named your problem is simpler in some ways. Look to the chapter, "Booklets, Bulletins, Leaflets," for special advice.)

4. *Estimate the number of lines of type and the number of words you will probably be able to use for those directions.* Now go back and rewrite those steps, trying to get the word count down to fit the space without sacrificing clearness.

You will undoubtedly have to do this over and over. As you work, examine each word, each phrase, to see that it expresses clearly and simply the action involved. Substitute short, simple words for those long, pretentious ones; short sentences for long, involved ones. Weed out technical terms that have meaning for a manufacturer but not for a homemaker.

5. *Try out your own rewritten directions.* Or better yet, get some inexperienced person to try them "cold," while you watch, answer questions, and make notes.

6. *Begin all over again, probably, and rewrite the whole thing.* Each time you work it over you will recognize real improvement. Keep on working until your directions are as foolproof and failure-proof and easy to follow as you can possibly make them.

Now, and now only, are you ready to retype your material neatly and show it to your editor or advertising manager, or whoever your boss may be.

Of course, the problem of getting women actually to read and follow your directions is not entirely solved by your writing those directions simply. Size and spacing of type, illustration, color and finish of paper stock all have a bearing on whether the woman is tempted to read the instruction sheet. But if your directions are clear in wording, friendly in tone, they are much more likely to be read and followed than if they are technical in wording, cold in tone.

The writing of directions carries heavy responsibilities. You, as a responsible home economist, will not write them carelessly.

WRITING COPY TO FIT SPACE

Many times — as in preparing a set of directions or a leaflet — you will be required to write copy to fit a specific space. If you are working with an artist, he will give you a layout to follow and a sample of the size and kind of type that is to be used. With these you can figure accurately how much to write. Here's how to proceed:

CHILD-TRAINING

If there are little folks around you, encourage them to learn to give clear, complete directions, as telling how to get to the market. Such training is fun for them; will help them in later years.

TOPIC SENTENCE!

In writing directions and/or recipes, you have a topic sentence already established, for you are writing about some narrowed-down idea.

1. Lay the sample of type on the layout and figure how many lines of type it is going to take to fill that space. Next, count every letter and every letter space between words in one of those lines. Write down that number. This is your "character count" per line.

2. Now set your typewriter to coincide with your character count per line and type your copy. At times it may be necessary to run two or three letter spaces over or under that designated count, but try to keep each line within your character count. When you are through typing your copy, count the number of lines that you have, then compare that number with the number of lines needed to fit the layout. All you need do now is to write more, or to cut back some of what you have written, to make the two coincide!

If you are not working with an artist, make a rough layout of your own. Then consult your printer as to the size and face of type that would be best to use. Ask him for a sample of that type, and proceed as has just been described.

If the printer has not yet been selected, look through magazines until you find a size and face of type that seems just right. Cut out a sample of it, lay it on your rough layout, figure character count per line, and count the number of lines required. When copy has been written to fit, show layout and type to the printer who eventually takes over the job. If he does not have that particular type face in stock, he will select one that is similar to your choice.

6.

Recipes

A refresher course
in writing food copy

ARE YOU a recent home economics graduate going into test-kitchen work? Or a not-so-recent one moving from teaching or dietetics or institutional foods into a business job in the food or kitchen equipment or home editorial field? Then you will probably find you have to adjust your ideas of recipe writing. For business home economists have long since learned that a recipe can and should be more than a standardized formula for making a standard product.

Unlike recipes used in the classroom, which have the benefit of personal introduction by the teacher, the recipe published in a newspaper or magazine or cookbook, or in a booklet or advertisement, or printed on a carton or can, must sell itself to readers or shoppers. If it does not, it might as well not be printed. (As a matter of fact might *better* not be printed, for such a recipe is a waste of expensive space.)

How can a recipe be taken out of the sterile formula classification and given real kitchen appeal? Let's put the problem into our mental mixers.

Writing a recipe is something like decorating a cake. It takes skill as well as know-how, plus a light, fresh touch.

In planning and writing a recipe for wide distribution, you have three hopes:

You hope every woman who *sees* the recipe will *read* it. You hope every woman who *reads* the recipe will *try* it. You hope every woman who *tries* the recipe will *like* it.

Before you do any actual writing, you will, of course, have to select — or adapt or originate — the right recipe for the particular purpose you have in mind. (And more about the need for "recipe inventing" in Chapter 8, "Ideas and Ingenuity.")

Selecting a just-right recipe is important. A recipe that would be suitable for editorial presentation in certain magazines may be too elaborate for use in an extension circular on nutrition. One that would be excellent to include along with others in a general recipe booklet may not have wide enough appeal to justify using by itself on a package label. An especially good recipe of limited appeal might appear in a general cookbook where there are many recipes from which to choose, but not be a good choice for use in a magazine. And so it goes.

Once you have chosen what you consider the right recipe for the situation, you are ready to figure ways and means of persuading homemakers to read, use, and enjoy your offering.

First, how can you tempt women to read your recipe? In a number of ways.

The *title* you give it can lead a woman to read that recipe eagerly, or turn her away.

Generally speaking, a recipe title should be sensibly descriptive rather than outlandishly novel. It should give at least some clue as to what can be expected of the finished dish. For example, "60-Minute Rolls" is a good appealing title because it tells something definite about the recipe; it promises something to the reader. "Yeast Rolls," on the other hand, is a mere label.

RECIPE FILING

Organize your recipe files to fit the needs of your department, rather than follow systems laid down by others.

TEMPORARY FILES

Along with a permanent file system, most home economists have a temporary one into which go recipes and ideas to be tried at some future time. Such files should be gone through frequently — for reasons too obvious to mention!

FILE GUIDE

The index of a general cookbook will serve as a guide in setting up almost any type of permanent filing system.

A title may well be fresh and in line with to-day's thinking and manner of speaking, but should never be too cute and tricky. "Wun'f'l Puddy" is a wun'f'l example of what not to do along that line. At the same time, a title certainly should not be completely dull and colorless, such as "Dried Fruit with Mush," or "Congealed Salad."

The *general appearance* of the recipe has a great deal to do with how many persons read it. If it looks like a recipe, the readership percentage goes up. Surveys show that recipes-which-look-like-recipes are excellent bait to entice women to read advertising or editorial columns. If it looks open and inviting — that is, if it is set in easy-to-read type, in good black or dark color that stands out clearly and sharply on the page — readership goes up. If it has an appealing, mouth-watering illustration, that helps too.

As a home economist you may not have complete say about these matters of layout and type and illustrations. But you can keep studying into those subjects, gathering evidence as to what women want along these lines. You can keep developing ideas and judgment. And you can express your convictions modestly but authoritatively whenever you have a good opportunity to do so.

Let's suppose, then, that you have decided upon your recipe. You are assured that it will be set up in attractive readable form. You feel you can count on its interesting the casual reader to the point that she will stop, look, and read it.

What can you do to get her to go the rest of the way, and try the recipe? What can you do to make sure that when she does try it, she will be successful and happy with it the very first time?

One thing is certain; if she is dissatisfied in any way the first time she tries your recipe, she is not likely ever to try it again — and may even be prejudiced against you or your company from that

**RECIPES FOR
CANS AND CARTONS**

There are times in recipe-writing when a fresh, newsy recipe is needed. There are other times when a simple, standard one is demanded. In writing a recipe to go on a can of pumpkin, for example, a good standard recipe for pumpkin pie is a "must." Preferably one that uses the entire contents of that particular size of can.

time on! You want her to like that recipe so well on first trial that she will make it over and over, get to thinking of it as "my recipe." If she does that, it will be your highest praise!

Here is where your skill as a writing home economist — or a home economics writer — comes in. You can write that outstanding recipe in an ordinary matter-of-fact, take-it-or-leave it manner. Or you can write it in a way that will prompt the casual reader to use it. That kind of writing is recipe magic — but it is magic you can learn.

Just keep in mind that the two simple ingredients which make the difference between a dull-sounding and a makes-you-want-to-cook recipe are *clearness* and *friendliness*. Both qualities have the same root: *thoughtfulness* for the woman who will (you hope) use the recipe in her own kitchen.

Once you learn this magic it will shine through in every recipe that you write, even though the recipe may, in the last analysis, be poured into the most rigid of molds!

Basic How-To's to Keep in Mind

If you are totally inexperienced in recipe writing, or if you feel that you can improve your technique, here are the important points to keep in mind.

No matter what form or style the finished recipe is to take (see pages 54 and 55 for samples and discussions of formats and styles), the first step always is to *think* the entire procedure through, step by step. In other words, *organize your thinking.* Once you get ingredients and method reduced to logical order, you can write the first draft of your recipe in whatever style you are to use.

In doing that first draft, you will, of course, observe the following rules.

LIST INGREDIENTS IN ORDER

Put down all ingredients, with their measurements, in the order in which they are to be handled or used. If some items need special preparation in advance, list them first, even though they are to be added toward the last. For example, in a cake recipe that calls for adding sifted dry ingredients to a creamed shortening-sugar-etc. mixture it is sensible and usual to list those dry ingredients first, so they can be measured, sifted, and set aside, ready to use at the proper time.

In an upside-down cake, it is important to list first the topping ingredients — butter, brown sugar, fruit, and nuts — so the pan will be sure to be made ready before the batter is mixed. In a fruit cake recipe, it is wise to list the fruits and nuts first, since all the dicing and chopping and slicing should be done before the actual cake mixing is begun.

INTERPRET THOSE INGREDIENTS

To help the woman follow your recipe without wasting time and effort, give as much information as is feasible in the ingredient list for each item. For example, perhaps your cake recipe calls for 2 eggs. If those eggs are to be beaten before they are added to the mixture, say 2 *eggs, beaten.* Better yet, say 2 *eggs, well beaten,* or *beaten with a fork,* or whatever stage of beating is recommended. If, however, your list of ingredients is over-long, beating the eggs may be worked into the method, provided it does not slow it down.

In general, when tabulating ingredients, try to arrange procedures so the measuring of dry items comes ahead of the measuring of liquid or oily things. Try to make it easy for the woman to use the same cup or spoon without having to wash and dry it between usings. Few homemakers have du-

COST

All recipes are expensive to develop and bring to the homemaker. A poor recipe or a poorly written one is most expensive of all for it destroys the homemaker's faith in a company or a product. As one home economist puts it, "Remember, a lady's groceries are sacred."

CALORIE COUNT

It's well to look at each recipe from the standpoint of calories. If the dish is too highly caloric for many tastes, you can often soften that fact by suggesting low-calorie go-alongs.

plicate measuring cups and spoons, as test kitchens have!

When feasible to do so, group similar measurements of dry or liquid ingredients together, so that the woman does not have to shift back and forth from a cup to a half-cup, etc. For example, your recipe calls for ¼ *teaspoon cloves; 1 teaspoon cinnamon*; ½ *teaspoon nutmeg*; ¼ *teaspoon allspice.* A more sensible arrangement would present the teaspoon of cinnamon first, then the half-teaspoon of nutmeg, then the fourth-teaspoon each of cloves and allspice.

Incidentally, when spices, cocoa and the like are called for, it's smart to list those dark ingredients after the salt, soda, baking powder, etc., when feasible, so that the measuring spoons will not carry dark color into the white powders in the packages or cans.

Some of the recommendations given here admittedly represent ideals, rather than rules, and, for lack of space, cannot always be acted upon. But a recipe can be well written even though it must be kept short.

ORGANIZE THE METHOD STEP BY STEP

Begin by visualizing the prospective user standing in her kitchen, ready to try your recipe. Let's say it is a cake she is to make. What should she sensibly do first? Should she get out the pans and grease them? Turn on the oven to preheat? Then say so, right then and there. Don't wait until the end of the recipe to tell her something she should have known at the beginning. (Unless, of course, the number of words allowed you simply will not permit you to put such information there at the beginning where it belongs!)

Quantity recipes designed for use in institutional kitchens are a special problem. This problem is discussed at the end of this chapter.

Next, write down the steps necessary in putting those ingredients together. At this stage of writing, it will help you to number those steps to make doubly sure you outline the work in exact order of progression, with no back-tracking or criss-crossing. Make certain that you give the best order of work for the recipe in hand. Only thoughtful testing will prove that point.

Some directions call for fussy procedures. Some require unnecessary washing of utensils in combining ingredients. Instead of saying, for example, "*Beat egg yolks; wash beater, and beat whites stiff,*" why not make it, "*Beat egg whites stiff; set aside. With same beater, beat yolks,*" and then continue instructions.

UP-DATE YOUR METHODS

In figuring out and putting down the order-of-work in a recipe, give thought to present-day kitchen equipment. This is always something to watch for when you adapt an old recipe. If the long-baking casserole can be done equally well and perhaps in less time in an electric skillet, give the reader a choice of which utensil to use, giving cooking times in each case. If a batter or mixture needs a good beating, mention the approximate time required on the electric mixer or by hand. If a cake is particularly good for freezing, say so — if there is space for the words!

But use judgment. If you are young and inexperienced in living, you may have the feeling that all homemakers have the latest in kitchen equipment, because some of your young friends do. If you are one who has been working with recipes for a long time, you may, out of sheer inertia, go on using old methods, forgetting that times have changed. It's a matter of examining yourself as well as your recipes!

BE SPECIFIC BUT SENSIBLE

You will, of course, give such vital information as pan sizes, baking temperatures, cooking or baking times. When it comes to baking, however, it is well to allow some leeway to take care of variations in accuracy of oven regulators, differences in types and sizes and pans, and other factors. It's

MIS-PLACED!
These statements actually occurred in printed recipes: "*Place* several kinds of fruit through food grinder." "*Place* 2 packages frozen peas in saucepan." "*Place* in a large bowl 4 eggs, well beaten."

RECIPES AND GEOGRAPHY
Home economists are sometimes criticized for being too casual with recipe terminology as it relates to localities. "Southern Fried Chicken," for example, may suggest batter chicken to a good cook in Georgia and something else to one in Texas or Tennessee. Rather than be too specific, why not make it something like, "Oven-Fried Chicken with a Southern Accent?"

wiser to say, "Bake at 350° (moderate) 40 to 45 minutes, or until done when tested," or "Bake about 45 minutes, or until done," rather than be too exact about the number of minutes. If two minutes extra baking on a pan of cookies makes for an undesirable product, it's best to say, "*Bake 8 to 10 minutes. Do not over-bake.*"

Keep in mind that though your recipe says definitely, "Bake in an 8x8x2-inch pan," the woman who is making your cake may not have that size, so she glibly turns the batter into a 9x9x1¾ or a 10x10x1½-inch pan — and then she wonders why the cake is over-done in the time your recipe specifies! It does not occur to her that a 10-inch square pan has 36 square inches greater area than an 8-inch square pan, and that the batter spread out thus in a thinner layer will bake considerably faster. It does not occur to her that a cake which will be done perfectly in 30 minutes in a 350° oven when baked in a dull-finished aluminum pan, will require less time (or 25° lower heat) if baked in an enamel or glass or dark metal pan; *more* time if baked in a bright, shiny new pan. (Even if you publicize such pan facts over and over, the homemaker will pan the recipe if it turns out unsuccessfully for her. And even though you do use a just-right type of pan in your testing kitchen, that particular pan may not even be available in many homewares stores.)

The same general reasoning holds true for casserole baking and top-of-range cooking. The size of pan; the shape, deep or shallow; the material it is made of; whether or not the mixture has been refrigerated — all influence the length of cooking time and quality of results as well. While you cannot dictate the exact type of utensil a woman is to use, you can at least take the various probabilities into consideration in your writing. And you can tell whether or not to cover the utensil, and suggest using kitchen foil or a cooky sheet to cover a lidless casserole.

YOU NEED THESE DESK HELPS

"Handbook of Food Preparation" gives abbreviations and symbols, definitions and standards, weights and measures, purchasing guides, cooking time and temperatures and other valuable information. For your copy, send 50 cents to American Home Economics Association, 1600 20th Street N.W., Washington 6, D.C.

"Dimensions, Tolerances, and Terminology for Home Cooking and Baking Utensils." Published by American Standards Association, Inc., 70 East 45th Street, New York 17, N. Y. (Price 35 cents.)

"Canned Food Tables," outlining servings per container, together with nutritive values. Obtainable from Consumer Service Division, National Canners Association, 1133–20th St. N.W., Washington 6, D.C.

STATE NUMBER OF SERVINGS

Along with pan sizes, baking times, and temperatures, give the number of average servings to be expected from each recipe, or the number of muffins or cookies of a certain size, or the number of loaves of bread. Notice that *number of servings* is recommended rather than *number served*. The reason is obvious. A main dish which makes six servings may actually serve six persons under some conditions, or it may serve only two or three under other circumstances. Many variables enter in — the occasion, the rest of the menu, the appetites of the group.

These points — pan sizes, temperature, number of servings — are basic requirements for modern recipes. But you want your recipe to be far above standard in appeal and helpfulness.

TRY TO FORESEE PROBLEMS, QUESTIONS, AND DOUBTS

You are, for example, writing a steamed pudding recipe which calls for no eggs, no shortening. Foresee some homemaker's questioning, and tell her in advance that these are not necessary in that particular pudding.

You are writing a cake recipe which makes an unusually thin batter. Say so in the recipe, so that the woman who is making the cake for the first time will not conclude that it is a typographical error and decide to add more flour.

You are writing a recipe for meringues which calls for beating the egg whites to a certain stage before beginning to add the sugar. Don't just say, as many recipes do, "Beat until foamy," and let it go at that. What does foamy mean here? One inexperienced cook may take it that the whites should be beaten merely until they are sudsy-looking; another that the eggs should be beaten until stiff enough to stand alone. Foresee those inconsistencies, and be explicit.

If some procedure is vital to the success of the

SAY WHAT YOU MEAN: MEAN WHAT YOU SAY

Do you mean "1 cup cheese, grated" or "1 cup grated cheese"? "4 tablespoons shortening, melted," or "4 tablespoons melted shortening"? There's a difference.

Do you really mean "1 small minced onion," or "1 small onion, minced"? Is there such a thing as a minced onion? And is "mince" the best word for the purpose? Would "cut fine" describe the operation equally well? Many inexperienced cooks have no idea what "mince" means.

Do you really mean it when you say, "Pour batter into pan"? Some batters are thin enough to pour; others must be dropped or spread.

When deciding on a size or face of type to be used in recipes, be sure to study the common fractions in those sizes and faces. Fractions at best are hard to read. In many recipes that are otherwise distinct, the fractions scarcely register. Remember, many women have poor vision, work in poorly lighted kitchens.

In compiling r e c i p e s, avoid using 5/6 and 7/8 whenever possible. One young cook says, "When I see a recipe that calls for some strange fraction, I skip that recipe."

recipe, say so in one way or another. You may say simply, "*Stir hot liquid slowly into beaten eggs. This is important.*" Or, "*Be sure to stir the hot liquid slowly into the beaten eggs.*"

Once you're sure your recipe is clear, complete, and can be fitted into the allotted format and word count, stir in all the appeal possible by means of skillful rewriting and editing.

USE HOME KITCHEN LANGUAGE

In the final writing of your recipe, take an informal approach, if possible. If you remember that your recipe is supposed to be used in a home kitchen, you won't be so likely to go formal and superior in your writing.

When you study some of the most popular cookbooks, you find that many of the recipes begin with a line or so of interesting information about the recipe itself, or about the resulting dish. A recipe for a quick chocolate cake may begin, "If you melt the shortening and chocolate together in a large double boiler or a bowl set in hot water, you can mix this entire cake in one utensil." A fruit cake recipe may promise, "This recipe makes five pounds of rich, moist, dark fruit cake. If you prefer a light cake, simply omit the spices." Such introductory words not only give useful information, but they set the tone of the recipe as one of friendly informality and of kitchen reality.

In some places it is not feasible or necessary to use such selling lines to lead into your recipes. But where they do work in, they work well.

Whether you begin your recipe with a preamble or not, you will be wise to put an informal, me-to-you attitude into your writing. But don't over-use the word *you*, or the recipe may sound patronizing. If you keep the reader constantly in mind as you write, she is almost certain to feel that you are writing directly to her.

Work for a lively, interesting style of writing. Choose words that are as lively as yeast. Put them together in sentences that have the charm and appeal of fresh-baked rolls. Result: a recipe with that wonderful makes-you-want-to-cook quality.

What are lively words? First, of course, are the verbs — strong action verbs which give a definite picture of a process or an act. Weak, general verbs such as poor old overworked *add* and *place* can be replaced by dozens of others that much more clearly express the action you have in mind.

Second come the adjectives — colorful, pictorial adjectives which describe something in concrete terms. When you say, "These cookies are delicious," you create no mental picture of those cookies. But when you say, "This makes a firm, chewy cooky — just right for those lunch-boxes," you give the homemaker a preview of what she can expect. And you'll be surprised at how few words it takes to accomplish this in many recipes.

When you are searching your vocabulary for the most expressive word, try to find one that at the same time is simple, straight-forward, familiar to readers. Avoid long, involved words with strings of prefixes and suffixes dangling.

What are appealing sentences? First, they are simple and clear. They are not scrambled. They are not dripping with complex clauses and phrases. They are of varying lengths — mostly short and crisp, with enough longer ones included to make for smooth, easy reading and to avoid a choppy, bossy-sounding style. Short and long sentences are woven together into paragraphs with regard for rhythm, balance, and change of pace.

How can you develop that regard for smooth writing? How can you learn to turn out brisk but smooth sentences and paragraphs?

RECIPES FOR ADVERTISEMENTS

When you are to prepare a recipe for an advertisement, ask for a layout. Estimate space allowed, then select a recipe that can be written to fit that space. Some recipes simply cannot be reduced to small space without sacrificing clearness and goodness.

RECIPES FOR RADIO

When you write recipes that are to be broadcast, select those that have ear appeal. Keep to a minimum of ingredients— usually not more than six items for a recipe that is to be dictated over the air.

By reading and writing! Read and study recipes critically. Try to figure out just why one is pleasant to read, easy to follow; why another is jerky, difficult to understand. Notice that even such small points as the number of words in a sequence and the way they are arranged can make for smoothness or for awkwardness. Study punctuation, too. Modern writers use just as few punctuation marks as are absolutely necessary to make the meaning clear.

Then practice. Try different ways of saying what you want to say. Study your own writing critically. Don't hesitate to throw away what you have written and begin again. Sometimes you have to throw away several wastebasketfuls of discarded sentences and paragraphs to turn out a single really well written recipe.

NATIONAL APPROACH

If your recipes or other information are to be used nationally, make them fit various sections of the country. A booklet on using a pressure saucepan, for example, should include directions f o r cooking okra and artichokes and celery root, even though those vegetables are not commonly used in every section of the United States.

WATCH OUT FOR INCONSISTENCIES

There is more to good writing than choosing good words and composing good sentences. You have to be watchful about a number of points.

Remember to keep parallel points or items or words actually parallel in your writing. For example, you must not join nouns and verbs with the word *and*. Yet notice in how many recipes you read, "Add flour, salt, pepper, and stir." If you must save space, say, "Add flour, salt, and pepper; stir." The semicolon marks the end of the parallel units.

Watch to keep the same point of view throughout a recipe. If you wish to switch from second person to first person in order to tuck in an explanation (as you might appropriately in a personally signed article or cookbook), remember to enclose your direct remarks in parentheses, or otherwise set them apart.

THOSE PAN SIZES

Before you put out a recipe calling for a pan of a specific size, check to find out whether that size is in common use in home kitchens or is available i n m o s t housewares stores. Pans used in testing kitchens are not necessarily the sizes found in the average kitchen cupboard.

"We home economists might as well recognize the fact that while we can standardize recipes, we can't standardize the women who will use those recipes."

Watch tenses. Don't switch from present to past to present again in the space of one sentence or paragraph or recipe.

Adopt one style pattern and stick to it throughout the recipe or group of recipes. If you use numerals in one place, use them all the way through. Don't spell out a number in one line, use a figure in the next. If you set out to express measurements in cups, tablespoons, etc., use that style consistently. Don't say *cup* in one place and *cupful* in another. If you use abbreviations at all, use them all the way through.

If you are writing recipes for editorial use in a specific magazine, study the food articles in the current issue of the publication. Follow the recipe style which that magazine uses, whether it is your personal choice or not. Check on whether the recipes call for "Shortening, melted, 4 tablespoons," or "4 tablespoons melted shortening"; whether the word *teaspoon* is spelled out in its columns, or abbreviated *tsp.* or *teasp.*

You have to be consistent about actual measures, too. If you call for a definite amount of one item in a recipe, you must give definite amounts of all other items, otherwise the proportions may be thrown completely out of proportion. Violation of this rule is a common error in many cookbooks put out by local groups. It is common also in those folksy-sounding radio chatter recipes or recipe-ettes. The thoughtless writer airily dictates, "Just mix half a can of bouillon with tomato juice to make a marvelous appetizer." Why "half a can" of bouillon when nothing is said about how much tomato juice is to be used?

All these rather dull-sounding *musts* and *have to's* have a very real bearing on the enjoyment a woman will get out of using the recipes you write. Your observance of them demonstrates your

INSTEAD OF "ADD"

"Add" is such a convenient word! Because of its shortness, it is chronically overworked. When you are tempted to use it, stop and think, "Does 'add' convey the exact meaning here? Or would another expression better express the action?" One of these, for instance:

Pour into
Stir into
Drop in
Blend in
Combine with
Put in
Mix in
Beat in
Whip in
Toss in

Five Ways To Write A Recipe—

These are, of course, not the only ways to write a recipe, but they do illustrate the basic patterns most frequently followed in recipe writing. If you will examine thoughtfully each recipe that you read in advertising and editorial columns of newspapers and magazines for a period of a week or two, you will find examples of most of the recipe patterns given here, and various combinations and adaptations of them.

1.

This might be called the chronological pattern for recipe writing, for ingredients are called for as they are used. It's a bit on the dictatorial side, too — note that each sentence begins with a verb of command. Many young homemakers are partial to this pattern because they say it is easiest for them to follow.

Cheese-Frosted Biscuits

Melt together in double boiler:
   1 cake (3 ounces) pimiento cream cheese
   3 tablespoons butter or margarine

Sift: 2 cups all-purpose flour

Measure, then **sift** again with:
   3 teaspoons baking powder
   ½ teaspoon salt

Cut in with pastry blender:
   4 tablespoons shortening

Add: ¾ cup milk

Stir only until flour is dampened. **Turn out** onto lightly floured canvas or board, and **knead** lightly 20 to 30 seconds.

Roll or **pat out** ½ inch thick, cut with floured cutter and **place** close together on ungreased baking sheet. **Stir** melted cheese and butter until well blended, **top** each biscuit with a spoonful of the mixture, and **bake** in hot oven (450°) 12 to 15 minutes. Makes about one dozen 2-inch biscuits.

2.

The idea back of this "Traditional" or "Conventional" pattern for writing recipes is that the user will measure out all ingredients before beginning to put them together. Some women say they like this pattern best because they can check the list of ingredients at a glance, and see whether they have everything at hand. Some beginners say it is confusing to try to follow measurements in one place and method in another.

Cheese-Frosted Biscuits

   1 cake (3 ounces) pimiento cream cheese
   3 tablespoons butter or margarine
   2 cups sifted all-purpose flour
   3 teaspoons baking powder
   ½ teaspoon salt
   4 tablespoons shortening
   ¾ cup milk

Melt cheese and butter together in double boiler. Sift flour, measure, then sift again with baking powder and salt. With pastry blender cut in shortening, until mixture looks like coarse crumbs. Add milk, stirring only until flour is dampened. Turn out onto lightly floured canvas or board and knead lightly 20 to 30 seconds. Roll or pat out ½ inch thick, cut with floured cutter, and place close together on ungreased baking sheet. Stir melted cheese and butter until well blended, top each biscuit with a spoonful of the mixture, and bake in hot oven (450°) for 12 to 15 minutes. Makes about one dozen 2-inch biscuits.

3.

Recipes written according to the conventional pattern need not be coldly impersonal as a chemical formula, though they are often just that. Here is a conventional-type recipe, condensed to fit an advertising or editorial layout, but brought to life by its informal, conversational style of writing.

CHEESE-FROSTED BISCUITS

Turn on oven to preheat to 450° (hot). Melt together in double boiler, stirring occasionally:

1 cake (3 ounces) pimiento cream cheese
3 tablespoons butter or margarine

Make baking powder biscuits as you usually make them, using 2 cups packaged biscuit mix, or your favorite recipe. Roll them rather thin (about 1/3 to 1/2 inch), cut with small cutter, and place close together on ungreased baking sheet. Top each biscuit with a spoonful of the cheese mixture, and bake 12 to 15 minutes. Serve hot, with salad. It is not necessary to serve butter with these. Makes about one dozen 2-inch biscuits.

4.

This adaptation of the conventional or traditional recipe pattern, with each step in the method plainly numbered, was developed to satisfy those inexperienced cooks who complained that it was difficult to follow directions when run together in a solid paragraph. In writing recipes according to this pattern, begin each step with an action verb.

Cheese-Frosted Biscuits

1 cake (3 ounces) pimiento cream cheese
3 tablespoons butter or margarine
2 cups sifted all-purpose flour
3 teaspoons baking powder
1/2 teaspoon salt
4 tablespoons shortening
3/4 cup milk

1. Melt cheese and butter together in double boiler.

2. Sift flour; measure, and sift again with baking powder and salt.

3. Cut in shortening, using pastry blender.

4. Add milk, stirring only until flour is dampened.

5. Turn out onto lightly floured canvas or board, and knead lightly 20 to 30 seconds.

6. Roll or pat out 1/2 inch thick, cut with floured cutter, and place close together on ungreased baking sheet.

7. Stir melted cheese and butter until well blended, and top each biscuit with a spoonful of the mixture.

8. Bake in hot oven (450°) 12 to 15 minutes. Makes about one dozen 2-inch biscuits.

5.

Here is a "Chattered" recipe (i.e., set up without tabulating the ingredients) done in extremely chummy, explanatory style. As given, a great many words and lines are necessary. Figure where and how you might cut the recipe and still retain the chattered style.

CHEESE-FROSTED BISCUITS

First turn on the oven to preheat, setting the control at 450° (hot). Put into a double boiler a 3-ounce cake of pimiento cream cheese and 3 tablespoons butter or margarine, and let melt, stirring occasionally. While this mixture is melting, sift some all-purpose flour onto a sheet of waxed paper. Measure 2 cups of this sifted flour, spooning it lightly into the measuring cup so it won't pack; level off the top with the straight edge of a knife or spatula. Put the measured flour back into the sifter, add 3 teaspoons baking powder and 1/2 teaspoon salt, and sift together into a mixing bowl.

Now drop in 4 tablespoons (that's 1/4 cup) shortening, and with a pastry blender or 2 knives, chop-chop that shortening with the flour until the mixture looks like coarse crumbs. (Leaving the shortening in bits this size makes for flakiness in the finished biscuits.)

Add, all at once, 3/4 cup milk, and stir with a fork just until flour is dampened and mixture holds together fairly well. Turn out onto a lightly floured canvas or board, and knead gently 20 to 30 seconds. (This kneading makes for smooth, well-shaped biscuits.) Roll or pat out 1/2 inch thick — or even less — and cut with a small cutter, dipping it in flour frequently so dough won't stick to it. Place the biscuits close together on an ungreased baking sheet. Stir the melted cheese-and-butter mixture again, and spoon it lightly over the biscuits. Bake in hot oven (450°) about 12 minutes, or until nicely browned and done. Makes about two dozen tiny biscuits, superb to serve with salad or with practically anything. It is not necessary to serve butter with these.

thoughtfulness for the eventual user, just as do your thinking-out of the logical steps and your inclusion of explanatory notes and warnings.

USE COMMON SENSE ALWAYS

While strict accuracy is vital to success in many recipes, there are other, more casual recipes in which absolute accuracy is neither vital nor advisable. The more you learn about cooking and about women's cooking habits, the more reliable your judgment will become as to where you must be precise, and where you can and should be more free and easy.

For example, in a perfectly balanced cake recipe, it is often necessary to call for rather elaborate fractional measurements, such as "¾ cup plus 2 tablespoons" sifted cake flour.

In a recipe for something like stuffed pork chops, however, it seems rather absurd to get into fine fractions in stating the amounts of bread crumbs needed. Instead of calling for "1¾ cups fine dry bread crumbs" to stuff 6 chops which are certainly not standardized, wouldn't it be more sensible to call for "2 cups"?

In a recipe for Waldorf salad, instead of calling for "1½ cups diced apple," wouldn't it be more in line with good home kitchen practice to say, "Allow 1 medium-sized tart apple for each 2 servings"?

In a recipe for pudding sauce, instead of calling for precisely "2¼ teaspoons sherry," wouldn't it be more sensible to say, "2 to 4 teaspoons sherry, or simply, "sherry to taste"? In recipes with which some liberties can safely be taken, isn't it better to give the reader some basis for forming her own judgment, rather than to give arbitrary amounts of items which can and should be varied to suit family tastes and ideas?

WHAT MAKES IT DELICIOUS?

There are synonyms for delicious, of course, but what quality expresses its appeal or your reaction more specifically? Is it tangy, piquant, spicy, tart, savory, mellow, zesty, frosty, refreshing, cool, colorful, fruity, juicy, nutty, buttery, sweet, rich, hearty, satisfying, wholesome, filling, delicate, dainty, tender, crisp, crispy, crusty, crunchy, chewy, creamy, whipped-creamy, intriguing?

Queries About Quantity Recipes

Why do so many excellent large-quantity recipes that have been developed and tested so carefully and printed so expensively go unused in institutional kitchens?

To answer that question and to figure out a constructive approach to wider acceptance of quantity recipes, a bit of visualizing and analyzing is in order. Yes, and a bit of dramatizing — that is, bringing to life of the writing of those stiff-looking formulas.

First step in inviting food service managers to try a quantity recipe is to give it a fresh, interesting title. Second — and this is rarely done — is to supply a few words of description that will enable the manager or head cook to visualize the dish. If a good photograph can accompany the recipe, so much the better are its chances of being read and tried.

Third step is to set the recipe up in an easy-to-follow typographical form. Should your recipes be on cards or in a booklet? Votes seem to be about evenly divided between 4x6-inch file cards, and booklets of approximately that size. But something more is needed.

In the effort to make a recipe look and sound completely standardized and professional, it is well to remember that human beings, not automated machines, are to use it. The men and women who work in institutional kitchens vary greatly in professional training and experience, and in their ability to read and understand printed English. Some find it difficult to interpret and follow a rigid formula — at least for the first few trials.

Take the cooks who prepare lunches for school children. Whether they are volunteers or paid workers, are not most of them homemakers, learn-

LESSON FROM A VIOLIN

It is possible for one to understand music and to know the principles involved in playing a violin, and yet not be able to play one very well. To do so takes practice. The same is true in writing recipes.

If the recipes you have written seem to be awkwardly stated, try reading them aloud. This will help you to get a better rhythm; make the recipes more pleasing to follow.

If even after long practice in writing recipes yours seem weak and ineffective, take a course in basic English. Many a beginning home economist needs to do just that.

ing to multiply home cooking skills by 50 or 150? Might it not be wise to soften the stiffness of those mathematical formulas with some of the cautions and reassurances that women appreciate in home-size recipes?

Types of recipes welcomed by restaurants, of course, differ markedly from those designed for schools and institutions who serve "captive customers." But the same need for clear writing exists. A recipe should be so clear and complete, so easy to understand, that one of the helpers in kitchen, pantry, or bakeshop department can follow it with no problem of interpretation.

Which brings up another point.

Institutional departments of most business firms do give both weights and measures of most ingredients in their quantity recipes. But there are still some gaps.

Eggs, for example, in large kitchens often are measured by cups, pints, or quarts rather than by count or weight. (Hard-cooked eggs, of course, would be called for by count.) But when more than 3 or 4 eggs are called for in a recipe, both measure and weight might well be given. (As "1 pint eggs [1 pound]" or "1½ pints egg yolks, [1½ pounds]" or "1 quart egg whites [2 pounds].")

Granulated sugar, also, often is measured by quarts, pints, and cups rather than by weight. Milk, water, and other liquids are probably more likely to be measured than weighed. To play safe, give both measure and weight. And, wherever possible, avoid complicated fractions, such as "2⅞ cups."

Much good work has been done toward standardizing quantity recipes. Now it would seem time to go a step further, and bring those recipes to life — for the good of the kitchen help, the customers, and, of course, the firm which is putting out those recipes!

First, last, and at all times keep visualizing the homemakers who will use your recipes.

7.

Menus and Meal Plans

How to build up
appetites with words

IF YOUR WORK INCLUDES recipe-writing, you will at times need to round out those recipes by suggesting what to serve with them. Such meal plans may take the form of a sentence or two at the end of the recipe. Or they may be made into actual menus-that-look-like-menus.

When your recipe is planned for a simple home meal, the first form is usually preferred. If it is to accompany a more formal or elaborate dinner, the second form may be better. In either case, the layout or amount of space available is a determining factor.

Whatever form the menu may take, always consider how that meal plan will fit into the time schedule and the budget of the homemaker. Check its value nutritionally. Give a thought to balance of flavors, temperatures, textures, colors, and to sensible calorie count. Visualize the serving of the meal — yes, and the dish-washing that follows it. These are all basic problems in the lives of women at home. Ask yourself will it be easy or difficult to manage the cooking of the various

A menu is a picture of a meal. It can — and should — have meaning, as well as artistry.

items, so that they are ready for the table at the same time? Show the homemaker that you understand her problems when you tell her what to serve!

How do you give meal suggestions appetite appeal? By using simple, mouth-watering words and phrases, and seeing to it that the menu makes sense to the women who will use it.

Menus for Restaurants and Tea Rooms

At some time in your home economics career you may be working with or for restaurants or other public eating places. A part of your job may include writing menus. If so, your technique will be quite different from that used in writing for homemakers.

First, mentally probe the minds and habits of the customers. They're not concerned with kitchen management; their sole interest is in getting something they like to eat at a price they are willing to pay. Menus designed to appeal to them should use pictorial words, rather than abrupt take-it-or-leave-it lists of dishes served.

In a popular restaurant, for example, "Ham" becomes "Baked Ham with Pineapple Garnish." "Green Salad" is listed as "Tossed Green Salad with Roquefort Dressing." In a restaurant known for its gourmet foods, however, more elaborate terms may be used. Important thing in each instance is to use appetizing, picture-suggesting words, without overdoing it. Beware of promising more glamour than the restaurant kitchen is equipped to furnish!

Menus for School Cafeterias

Visualize those moving rows of boys and girls, or older students, pushing their way toward the food center, intent on finding something they like

RECIPE ROUND-OUT

Whenever you write a recipe, see if it isn't possible to add at least 1 or 2 lines to suggest what to serve with that dish. Makes the recipe "taste" better in type and be more useful in the kitchen. No, you need not suggest the entire meal—perhaps just the right salad to round out a casserole dinner.

and can eat in a hurry, at a bargain price! The menu you put on the bulletin board or black-board is important in the lives of those boys and girls, and it is important that it be planned and written with care and friendliness.

Part of your job is, of course, to work with the preparation center. Part of it is to encourage youngsters to eat what is good for them. Part of it is to keep all concerned good-natured and happy. How do you achieve the latter? By punctuating the menu with an occasional smile.

One school cafeteria with a surplus potato problem, stepped up mashed potato sales by offering a plate called "Hot Dogs in a Snowbank." Another, finding the cooky stand at a standstill, introduced "Flying Saucer Cookies" that have been in demand ever since.

The fun touch! Keep it alive, especially when you are dealing with the lively young!

Menus for Institutions

When you work with a captive audience, one of the big appeals is freedom of choice. In writing hospital menus, for example, work in choices whenever feasible. Even those patients whose desserts are limited to gelatin like the idea of being able to specify the color and flavor!

Nutrition-Centered Meal Plans

It is good nutrition education to always round out a family-type menu with a discreet line here and there, pointing up some nutrition fact or reminder. The homemaker reads that recipe-with-menu before she has completely decided to try it. The way in which such nutrition lines are worked into the recipe and/or menu may influence her decision to try or not try the recipe.

If the eat-this-because-it's-good-for-you point of

MEAL HIGH SPOTS

One advertising executive reasons this way: If you want to "sell" an elaborate or expensive dessert, suggest a simple, low-cost main course to precede it.

view is emphasized above the eat-this-because-you'll-enjoy-it angle, some homemakers may react against it. Perhaps a compromise is needed at times. It may be possible, for example, to give the recipe an appealing title, then comment casually that, *as you (the homemaker) can see,* the Corn-Crab Casserole is packed with protein. Better selling can often be done by suggesting that the homemaker *does* know something about good nutrition, and that the statement used is merely a reminder.

Certainly every home economist can do much to further the cause of nutrition through careful planning of meals and through skillful use of words in describing those meals. This is true whether the home economist uses nutrition terminology, or appetite appeal, or a combination of both.

REMEMBER MAMA

Young mothers want help with their meal planning —especially simple meals for company. In giving them this help, keep in mind (a) how inexperienced they are, and (b) how busy! Since there are millions of young mothers, why not more menus written with their needs in mind?

BAKING PAN ARITHMETIC

To compare the relative capacities of layer cake pans, remember these formulas from Junior High days: The area of a circle equals πr^2. The cubic contents of a cylinder equal area of base times depth.

And so, for a round layer pan 8 inches in diameter and 1¾ inches deep, you take the radius (4 inches); square it (16 square inches); multiply by 3.1416. Answer: area of bottom of pan is 50.265 square inches. (Call it 50.3) Multiply that by 1¾ (depth of pan). Answer: contents of pan, 88 cubic inches.

A round 9-inch layer pan has a bottom area of 63.62 square inches — practically the same as that of an 8-inch square pan (64 square inches). But the 9 x 1¾-inch round pan has a content of only 111.335 cubic inches, whereas the 8 x 8 x 2-inch pan holds 128 cubic inches.

How to convert those cubic-inch contents into cupfuls? Simplest way is to measure how many cups of water it takes to fill the pan! Having done so, it's smart to write that measure on the outside bottom of the pan, using fingernail enamel. How do you measure content of a tube pan with removable bottom. That's right — use rice instead of water to fill it. — G.A.C.

8.

Ideas and Ingenuity

There's great need for
"yeasty" thinking

WHEN YOU WORK under pressure, as you're sure to do at times, there is always the temptation to follow familiar patterns. To use and re-use the same recipes, the same lesson plans, the same demonstrations, the same photographic approaches.

Certainly, good recipes and sound ideas should not be discarded simply because they are no longer new. There are always young homemakers and students coming along to whom those established facts are "news." Even so, everything that has to do with communications needs to be frequently re-examined to bring it in line with changing situations.

Let's look at recipes. When an outstandingly popular one, such as Toll House Cookies, comes out of a test kitchen, it deserves to be republished frequently, as it has been, not only for the sake of young homemakers but as a reminder and convenience for older homemakers, too. That is true of many recipes. But there is also great need for originality and ingenuity in creating recipes. Unless you develop these assets, you, like your ideas, may soon be out of step!

*A fresh idea is the yeast
that leavens and livens
solid loaves of information.*

[63]

But, you ask, how does one go about developing originality? How does one "invent" a new recipe?

Perhaps it's simpler than you realize.

The R/C System for Originating Recipes

It is true, of course, that all so-called new recipes have their roots in old established ones. But it is equally true that new twists and fresh adaptations can always be figured out for old-time favorites.

Suppose you are working in the canned foods field, and this week you are expected to develop some special uses for red kidney beans.

Or you are on the staff of a home magazine; your assignment is to work out fresh ideas for outdoor meals — especially some new ways with ever-popular canned beans which would help to round out a grill-cooked meal in the garden. Canned kidney beans are, of course, one of the types of beans you will feature.

Or you are a nutritionist, seeking as always to help your public to have more of the protein they need, in forms that are convenient to use and not too expensive to buy. You know that canned kidney beans live up to those requirements, and that they are generally liked. You know, too, that a good recipe will be more effective than any amount of nutrition-talk as such in encouraging homemakers to use more beans.

Whichever one of those home economists you may be, you are faced with the same dismaying thought: Surely every possible use for kidney beans has already been exploited! But has it?

Let's start with the known — the product and problem — and let our minds roam into the known or little known. Let's try inventing a new recipe featuring canned kidney beans.

Try putting the problem into your Unconscious, and turn it over from time to time. Don't be surprised if out of the blue comes the memory of the jelly bean candies you liked as a child. This is your key.

"Why not a Jelly Bean Salad?" you ask yourself. That is, a bean salad in gelatin. You like the idea. You are amused by the name. And you go to work on it, realizing all the while that the idea may or may not be workable.

First on the agenda is to think what would be needed to make beans-in-gelatin taste good and look attractive. Again your Unconscious may remind you of the bean salads frequently served in Italian restaurants — those appetizers made by mixing kidney beans or lima beans with chopped onion, mashed garlic, vinegar, and seasonings. It occurs to you that you might stir such a bean mixture into gelatin and mold it.

With that established, start on your recipe. Go at it first in a free-hand creative way. Drain and rinse the beans, then stir up your onion-garlic-vinegar-bean mixture, tasting as you go. Let stand while you make a batch of lemon-flavored gelatin, cutting down the liquid to balance the addition of vinegar, of course. Then stir the two together while the gelatin is still warm. When the salad is chilled and firm, test it, taste it — then go on to perfect your recipe.

When your idea has jelled literally, you may decide it is worth having its picture taken. This time you may chill the salad mixture in a ring mold, and serve it filled with cottage cheese, garnished with cucumber and radish slices.

Whatever direction your idea eventually takes, you will be rather pleased with yourself because you have created a practical new recipe that homemakers will enjoy using again and again.

If you're working with a particular food product and find fresh ideas slow in coming, try out the advice given by an outstanding woman in the advertising field.

TO SPARK AN IDEA

The primitive way to start a fire is to rub two sticks together until a spark is struck. To spark an idea, rub an open mind against a problem.

Good homemaking information, like convenience foods and drip-dry clothing, is in step with the times.

LOOK TO TV

When you study television commercials, you realize that back of every one of them there is ingenuity, fresh thinking. That is why those commercials are remembered; why they influence the thinking of homemakers — and of children!

In a speech before a large group of home economists she said (among other things): "It's easy to get new ideas. You just ask questions and turn things inside out, or backwards, or upside down . . . Change the size . . . Change the flavor . . . Change the color . . .

"If it's a dessert, maybe it could be a first course or a salad. If it's a vegetable, perhaps it can make a full meal, or be served as a snack. . . . Could your product make something simpler — as soup makes an easy gravy or sauce? If it's usually sweetened, try adding salt; if it's usually salted, try sugar." And so on and on.

In other words, look at your product with fresh eyes. Eventually your eyes may return to rest on a familiar and accepted way of doing, but somewhere along the line you will have freshened your approach, so that the old familiar takes on new interest for you and your homemakers.

Ingenuity is not limited, of course, to creating new recipes for publication. The same mental processes produce fresh ideas along any line.

Often ingenuity is prompted by necessity or thrift. For example, the need for several large flower vases for a Mother's Day reception in one school suggested this artistic solution. Tall tin cans were neatly covered with newspaper classified advertising pages, giving the effect of interesting texture and design.

Frequently it is sparked by spontaneity. One student in child development started a chain of teaching fun by showing a preschooler a picture of a telephone in a magazine advertisement, and letting him "call up" his friends. So much more range for his imagination than either a real or toy phone could give!

Ingenuity can also be the starting point of discoveries. "What would happen if —" is often the magic line that leads to more interest in learning and in teaching.

(P.S. That Jelly Bean Salad is really good!)

A TEACHER SPEAKS UP

"I found my sewing class took on new interest when I suggested that each bring to class some worn or out-of-style garment for group discussion as to what might be done to make it wearable. Those students showed more ingenuity than I had thought possible."

9.

Information Releases

How to meet the
editor's requirements

CHANCES ARE that as a home economist in business or extension, you will find yourself responsible for preparing regular or occasional information releases for use by newspapers.

What is a release?

In this connection it is thought of as a brief article on a single subject, planned and written in such a way that it can be reproduced in the homemaking sections of daily or weekly newspapers.

Why such releases?

They are designed to spread the word about new and worthwhile ideas, methods, or product uses. The underlying aim is, of course, to interest homemakers in investigating and trying the food or household product that is involved.

Such releases may take the form of a semi-exclusive article (with or without photographs) for city newspapers, or they may be done in mat form to fit the needs of small-circulation papers. They may be sets of mimeographed or printed pages from which the editor selects the recipe she wishes

*Before your recipe release
can reach the homemaker,
it must go through
the Food Editor's sieve!*

to feature and requests the photograph to accompany it. They may be done as clip sheets filled with brief paragraphs.

Whatever the format (which is usually dictated by one's company or association or advertising agency) the object of any release is to have it reach as many readers as possible. The advantages and disadvantages of each type of release, as to cost, flexibility, and other factors, must be debated within the company. Never is it left to a young, inexperienced home economist to decide such a weighty problem all by herself.

When there is more than one daily newspaper in a metropolitan area, the foods page editor of each paper quite naturally demands an exclusive release, entirely different in idea and handling from those offered the other papers in the area.

Most syndicated writers on food or homemaking subjects utilize some release material from business home economists. Like the metropolitan dailies, they expect "exclusives."

Planning and preparing good, usable releases, regardless of subject matter and format, require some special know-how, special techniques. But these are not too difficult to acquire. Help is given in the pages that follow. And if you are very inexperienced, you'll find that food editors and experienced heads of home economics departments are happy to help a beginner learn the ropes of this specialized type of writing. Don't be hesitant about asking for help.

Before exploring techniques, visualize the home department editors to whom your release will be hopefully offered. What are their problems, their requirements?

Every homemaking editor has one big aim: to pack the columns of her department with fresh, dependable recipes, useful information, and new ideas, all presented in ways that will attract and hold the homemaker's attention and tempt her to action.

Every editor is faced with the problems of space and of time. She has room in her pages for only a small percentage of the stories and pictures the mail-boy piles on her desk each week. And she rarely has time to rewrite an awkwardly written story, even though the idea in it is well worth using.

Your offering must compete with those dozens of other releases for the editor's approval before it has a chance of reaching her readers.

The more editors you get to know personally, and the more you read and study homemaking pages in newspapers and other publications, the better insight you will have into what editors want to publish and readers like to read.

Your work, then, is cut out for you. Your question is, "Where do I start?"

Let's discuss the recipe release first, since more releases of this type are distributed than of any other one kind. They are issued not only by processors or packers of food products and associations of food producers, but by manufacturers of large and small appliances, utensils, and gadgets used in home preparation of foods.

Start with Fresh Thinking

First of all, figure out a good recipe-idea — one that will do something for your product because it will do something for homemakers. Better yet, think up an assortment of possible ideas from which to choose.

Such recipes must be fresh and newsy to appeal to editors and their readers. They must come through quickly and clearly in words and photographs.

They must be soundly practical from the homemaker's point of view — not too expensive, too elaborate, too exotic. They must not call for unusual supplies and special skills which the run-of-the-kitchen homemaker doesn't have. Yet they must not be too plain and ordinary!

Getting a recipe-idea that lives up to all those musts is not a matter of merely picking one out, but of thinking one out. That is hard work. It calls for mind-digging, not just thumbing through the

WHAT IS NEWSWORTHY?

An idea may be fresh and interesting, yet not have enough depth to be really worth publicizing. When you have figured out something you think might make a release, it's wise to write it out, set it aside a few days, then read it objectively. For further testing, try it out on someone (your boss, perhaps) who can be counted on for a sensible and frank opinion.

files for "something that will do." At first you may feel completely baffled. But put your mind seriously to work, and you'll find you *can* think out a new and different answer to some common problem of homemakers. Never be guilty of taking an old standard recipe and substituting your food product for the one usually called for.

It's encouraging to know that originality can actually be cultivated. Just keep practicing! You'll be surprised at the ideas you are able to generate. It's encouraging, too, to realize that often the problem itself prompts an original solution. (Remember the Jelly Bean Salad in Chapter 8.)

Work for a Strong Lead Paragraph

Now that you have worked up three or four fresh ideas and have developed them into good recipes, select the best one. Narrow the "selling point" of the recipe-idea down into a single sentence. Look at it. Would that sentence be a good one to lead off with? If not, how will you begin your story?

The important thing is to make that first sentence, that first paragraph, a forecast of what your story is about. Don't stall around with a lot of pointless words that lead the reader away from rather than into the story. Discussions of log fires and candlelight as a preamble to a recipe for bean soup or bread pudding is evidence that either an amateur or an old-fashioned writer has turned out the piece.

Take a tip from the jet pilot. Make sure you are all set to go, then get off the ground fast, and move right along.

You may center your lead on your big idea or you may swing it around and apply the idea to the homemaker, using that wonderful little word, "you." Whichever way you start out, keep that homemaker always in your mind. After all, she is the one you hope ultimately to reach.

MAKE IT CLEAR

In sending out any food release, make it clear that the recipes have been tested by a qualified home economist. Make clear whether or not the release is exclusive. See that the source and date are stamped on the back of every publicity photo.

NEWSLETTERS

Many foods editors look forward to receiving breezy newsletters from home economists in various fields. Such letters contain not only news of some product, but make good reading as well. There's a knack to writing these — a knack that can't be described but that can be learned.

Now follow up that lead with your recipe or recipes. Include such things as warnings and comments, if needed, or suggestions as to how to serve the dish or what to serve with it, or other helpful notes. But beware of letting the copy grow too long and wordy!

Write in Newspaper Style

Study newspaper foods pages. Use them as guides in figuring the length your recipe release should be. Count the actual number of words in some of those typical recipe stories. You will find that few recipes exceed 100 words.

Use plenty of verbs. Remember you are doing more than merely giving women a recipe. You hope to entice them into putting that recipe to work in their own kitchens. Verbs can help you to do just this.

Choose meaningful words, not empty ones. Make every word count. Specialize in short, uninvolved sentences averaging not more than 17 words each. Use brisk, short paragraphs, preferably not more than 5 to 7 newspaper-lines long. Watch particularly that your lead paragraph does not exceed the line limit.

Edit Your Copy Sharply

When you have written your recipe release as well as you think you possibly can, set it aside to "get cold." Then go back over it. You'll be amazed to see how much still needs to be done to make it strong and good. Don't for a minute take the attitude, "Oh, well, the head of the department will rewrite it anyway, so why should I struggle any longer!"

Instead, study it paragraph by paragraph, sentence by sentence, phrase by phrase, word by word.

Reread that lead paragraph. How does it sound

PUT IN MORE "WHY'S"

In writing all types of product releases, tuck in an occasional "reason why" a particular process is important. The editor will appreciate your doing this — provided the additional words do not make the copy too long.

compared with other recipe leads in the food section of your newspaper? Is it better than most of them? If not, try a different approach.

Are some of your sentences long and unwieldy? Cut them up into shorter ones. Are some of those words empty, meaningless generalities? Replace them with words that convey the exact meaning you have in mind.

Finally, consider the title of your story. It need not be written as a newspaper headline, but it should sound newsy and inviting.

Use Worthwhile Photographs

Are you including a photograph with your release? Make certain that it gets across one interesting idea. Make certain it is dramatic. Avoid heavy colors and shadows that come out black in newspaper print. Make it live up to the standards of good photography discussed in Chapter 3.

When is it wise to include a photograph with a release and when is it better not to do so?

There is no ready-made answer to this question. Common sense tells one that it is a waste of money to send photographs to publications that do not wish to go to the expense of having cuts made. Such papers may, however, be quite willing to use releases without photographs. Observation tells one that for metropolitan newspapers, photographs should usually or occasionally accompany releases. In general it is better not to send a photograph than to send one that does not measure up to standard. Here, again, frequent and frank conversations with newspaper food page editors will guide one as to what and what not to do.

What About Other Types of Releases?

Much of what we've discussed applies not only to writing the recipe release, but to all releases,

TIMING

Send out holiday ideas early — at least six weeks in advance. In writing timed releases, try to stretch their seasonal use. Make a holiday turkey release fit not only Thanksgiving, but the winter season of home entertaining. Just suggest the holiday season in general, without pin-pointing it to Thanksgiving, Christmas, or New Year's Eve.

ASK THE FOOD EDITOR

Most food editors of city newspapers receive hundreds of phone calls, asking questions on a variety of subjects. In talking with editors, find out what types of questions homemakers are asking. This gives you a clue to current homemaking interests and trends.

regardless of subject matter. Now for a closer look at those other types.

THE COLUMN

If you are a county home advisor in extension work or a district home economist with a utility company, you are likely to be faced with putting out a weekly or monthly release in the form of a signed newspaper column. In such a column you have the advantage of continuity, but you also have the problem of finding something new and interesting to write about each time. By keeping a notebook and jotting down questions and comments of homemakers you will never run out of fresh ideas from which to select!

There are two ways to approach writing a column feature. You may do each one as if you were writing a brief article for a magazine, swinging the entire column around one subject. (The marginal notes about writing for magazines — page 117 — will provide some guidance on this.) In other instances your column may be made up of short or longer paragraphs on a variety of related subjects, written in chatty, informal style. All newspaper column features will be something of a guide as to format and style.

"FILLERS"

If you are working with a nonfood product or appliance — one in the home laundering or household cleanser classification, for example — you have a specific problem, because trade names of products and equipment are not ordinarily used in newspaper columns.

Whatever releases you do along this line will probably consist of short but helpful household notes, free from trade names, which can be tucked in as "fillers" on the homemaking pages. The more such fillers can be made timeless, the better. If an editor has had a number of such shorts

FILLERS AND FACT SHEETS
Every filler that you send to an editor should contain a worth-printing idea put into the fewest words possible. It is the custom to send several such fillers at one time, so that they can be set in type and used when space permits.

set in type, she likes to select one that fills an exact spot. She prefers not to stop and weigh whether or not it is suited to the season.

In addition to preparing such fillers, you may very well need to do a sort of broadside information release about your product and its usefulness, to be sent to home economics teachers, magazine and newspaper editors, and home economists in public utility companies and other related fields. Such fact sheets should be complete, yet broken down so that the information is easy to read.

DOUBLE CHECK

Be sure that recipes in your product release are absolutely right. When checking the copy, check ingredient list against method, and vice versa, to make sure that each item listed is accounted for, and each item mentioned is listed in the ingredients.

Spotlighting the New Product

Your company is putting a brand new product on the market. It may be a new fast-cooking rice or a new type of rolling pin, a new detergent or a new dish-washer. Your job is to publicize such facts and relate them to the lives of people. Here you do it by writing straight news releases, following these rules:

First, before you begin writing the actual story, make a list of all the important points about the product. Sort them mentally. What is the big idea — the big news? Which points will have the greatest meaning and appeal for readers generally?

Put the important idea, the strongest points of interest, in your lead paragraph. Say what you have to say in a lively way, not in dull statements of dull facts. You are enthusiastic about the product, you feel others will be when they know about it. Work to communicate that enthusiasm in subtle ways — not by "rave" comments.

Keep the homemaker always in mind in preparing product releases. If food prices are high, or if there is a hint of hard times in the air, give her recipes that are thrifty but good. At holiday time when she feels like splurging, give her fancies that will make meals glamorous.

Tell the news simply. Keep the story, the paragraphs, the sentences short.

Along with the news story, it's a good idea to send a fact sheet or fact file about the new product, for future reference by the editor.

The recommendations for writing news about a new product apply also to writing a release about some new finding in the field of research. The results of a survey of the breakfast habits of teen-agers; new conclusions regarding marriage failures or successes — this type of story likewise is handled as a news feature.

Here, again, begin the story with an arresting statement of or about the discovery or conclusion — not with a chronological account of the events leading up to it.

Then, in following paragraphs, develop or discuss the important and interesting points in the order that serves best for the particular subject.

Summing up. In any type of release make clear in the first paragraph what you are going to talk about . . . Get that first point across quickly . . . Give information in clear, complete, orderly fashion and in as brief form as is sensible . . . *Work for a friendly, informal, direct style of writing — one that makes for easy reading.* Avoid technical words and scientific phrases . . . Put up your release in a form that is easy to recognize, easy to clip and use . . . Send it out. If it is well received and rather widely used, your pattern must be a good one. If it is not used, figure out why. (Another time, try harder!)

So much for the planning and writing of the various types of product and information releases. Another and unrelated type of release has to do with publicizing an organization. This is discussed in Chapter 18.

NOTE TO EDITORS

Outstanding among newspaper food pages are those that tie good national releases in with local situations, local notes and recipes, so that every story seems to have been written especially for that particular paper and town.

Here's Something To Think About

Here is a list of a dozen criticisms which food editors make regarding some of the product releases that cross their desks. Do any of these criticisms apply to *your* material?

1. Too many recipes for complicated dishes —

HEADLINES
Headlines on product releases are important. Big thing is to promise something, rather than merely to state a fact or use catch phrases. When a photograph accompanies a release, it's a good idea to tie the headline into it. Helps bring the picture to life at first glance.

Before you criticize product releases written by other home economists, remember there may be problems b e h i n d the scenes the outsider does not know.

mixtures that would take a homemaker a lot of time to put together, and that her husband would undoubtedly rebel at eating if she did.

2. Too many ingredients, and too expensive and unusual ones called for. Most items listed should be available on average home kitchen shelves.

3. Too long, wordy introductions, ambling and rambling all around the subject, instead of leading directly into it.

4. Too long sentences — sometimes averaging as many as 40 to 50 words, instead of the recommended 17 or so. Too long paragraphs, also.

5. Too much raving in introduction; too lavish praise of the product or the dish in question.

6. Too technical terminology used — chef's terms or laboratory words in place of common kitchen language.

7. Too commonplace ideas, lacking in news value. Some reminder copy is acceptable if written from the news angle of the season or the weather or the like.

8. Too fancy, elaborate photographs, not in line with trends in modern living, and not suitable for good reproduction.

9. Too commercial.

10. Too old-style in terminology and methods.

11. Too long and too dull.

12. Too late. This is especially the case with seasonal or holiday ideas.

10.

Booklets, Bulletins, Leaflets

How to make them
brighter, more usable

ARE YOU LIKELY ever to have to prepare material for a booklet or leaflet? The answer is a decided *yes*. Yes, certainly, if you have anything to do with the advertising or promotion of food or equipment or other household needs. Yes, certainly, if you go into extension service. Yes, almost certainly, if you go into newspaper or magazine editorial work. It's well, then, as a home economist in any field to have a good understanding of the *how's* and *why's* of booklet planning and production.

But first a word about the physical make-up of these highly specialized small publications.

A *booklet* is, as its name indicates, a small book, with its pages — usually 16 or more — saddle-stitched or stapled together. A *bulletin*, as issued by government bureaus and extension services, is actually a booklet.

A *leaflet* or *folder* consists of a single large sheet of paper folded to form small pages, but not stitched.

A *circular*, in extension terminology, is something between a booklet and a leaflet. Its pages

A booklet or leaflet, like today's household fabrics, can be bright and gay, yet completely practical.

**YARDSTICK
FOR A BOOKLET**

Every booklet should (1)
look or sound so interesting the homemaker will
want to *have* a copy. (2)
Be so interesting she will
want to *study* it. (3)
Have something in it that
will make the homemaker
want to *keep* and *use* it!

LEAFLET LAYOUT

To lay out a leaflet, fold
a sheet of paper to make
a dummy the exact size
your leaflet is to be. Seeing the small area on
each of those panels or
pages will help you to
write "lean"; will help
you spot recipes and ideas
so that every panel or
page "stops" the home-
maker — makes her want
to read what's there.

may be considerably larger than those of most
booklets and leaflets. Often it consists of just one
large sheet folded once, making four large, letter-
size pages. Sometimes it is made up of 8, or
possibly even 12 pages, loosely saddle-stitched together. Like the leaflet and folder it can be folded
flat and mailed in an ordinary business envelope,
whereas a booklet usually requires a special
envelope to fit and protect it.

All these small publications are alike in one
respect: Each is a unit, devoted to just one phase
of a big, general subject.

A good-sized booklet or bulletin, for example,
might discuss "Home Preservation of Fruits and
Vegetables," which is one fairly large segment of
the general subject of food preservation. In it
might be given directions for canning, preserving,
and freezing of fruits and vegetables. A smaller
booklet or circular would narrow the subject
down, perhaps to "Home Canning of Fruits and
Vegetables." A leaflet or folder would narrow it
down still further, perhaps to "How To Can
Tomatoes."

Or a good-sized booklet or bulletin might be devoted to "Planning the Farm Home Kitchen," a
definite segment of the general subject of home
planning. A smaller booklet or circular might discuss one phase of that segment, as, "Planning
Efficient Working Areas for Farm Kitchens." And
a still smaller leaflet or folder might confine itself to a still smaller phase of the subject, as
"Planning the Farm Kitchen Mixing Center."

When a booklet turns out to be large and comprehensive, covering many segments of a big
general subject, it is no longer a booklet, even
though it is paper-covered. It is a book.

The method of preparing a booklet or a bulletin
or a circular or any other sort of leaflet or folder
for publication is much the same. This holds
true whether the publication is 4 pages or 24;

whether the subject is foods or equipment or home management or home decorating or sewing; and whether the publisher is a business firm or a university extension office or a government bureau.

Let's consider first the putting together of a booklet or bulletin. To make it more concrete, let's say it is a recipe booklet for a food manufacturer. Once you have the general pattern from which to work, you can adapt it to fit any such assignment that comes along.

Where and How Do You Begin?

Before the job or any part of it is turned over to you, a number of points which hinge on company policy and budget plans will have been decided by the executives of your organization. You may be called in on the preliminary discussions of some of these points, or you may not. At any rate, when these decisions have been reached you will know definitely the general subject, the particular product to be featured, the basic purpose of the booklet, and the audience it is intended to reach.

You will know what size and shape the booklet is to be and the number of pages it will have. You will know what quality of paper stock is to be used; whether no color or two colors or four colors are possible; whether drawings or photographs or both are feasible. You will know who is to plan and lay out the booklet, who will supervise the production. You will know the publication date, and have a schedule of deadlines for copy, photos, first proofs, and final proofs.

With the specifications and limitations of the job outlined for you, it is time to get down to work in real earnest.

How do you begin? As always, by thinking.

Visualize and *analyze* — those two processes overlap, you know. You must visualize those

KNOW BEFORE YOU START

Discover what the mechanical problems or limitations are before you get too far in your planning. If your leaflet is to be mimeographed, talk with the girl who runs the mimeo. She can tell you what can and cannot be done. If you are working directly with the printer (without benefit of art direction) get his advice and ideas on layout and type. Saves time; makes for a better looking leaflet.

GOOD EXAMPLES

Study the homemaking leaflets and booklets put out by the agricultural extension service of your state. Many are splendid examples of what can be done at modest cost.

women who are to read and use and enjoy your as-yet-unwritten booklet. You must analyze their everyday problems pertaining to food, figure what you can put into the booklet that will help those women in solving those problems.

Think a minute about the *audience*. Of course "audience" is not, strictly speaking, the correct word, for audience implies hearing rather than reading. But it's a convenient way of referring to those readers you hope to have.

Are you to appeal to the tremendous group of middle-income and low-middle-income homemakers, or are you to aim at the relatively small group of upper-bracket homemakers? Are you expected to appeal to teen-agers, brides, experienced homemakers, or a cross-section of all these age-groups?

What Approach Will You Take?

What approach will please your audience most? A serious, straightforward one, or a light-hearted, amusing one?

Better think twice before going too far in the direction of amusement or whimsy or cuteness. Remember, too, that a serious, straightforward ings are fine in the here-today-gone-tomorrow type of printed matter, but they quickly become stale in a book or booklet that is used over and over. Remember, too, that a serious, straightforward approach need not and should not be a dull, heavy-handed one. Generally speaking, the approach of friendly but not bossy helpfulness is hard to beat — helpfulness in solving problems common to homemakers.

Many business-sponsored booklets are signed with the trade-marked name of the firm's home economist — a name which the firm has adopted to represent the composite personality of the entire home economics department, as Jean Porter, Patricia Collier, Betty Crocker, Marie Gifford,

When You're On Your Own

Find out or figure out what size type should be used in that leaflet or tear-off. From magazines cut paragraphs of type in corresponding size or sizes. Pin these onto your dummy, count the number of words, and be guided accordingly.

Martha Logan, Ann Pillsbury, Jane Sterling. In such an assignment you are free to write personally and directly to your readers, assuming the position of a recognized authority in your field. You are free to write in the first person — but you probably will not do so.

Recognizing that an entire booklet written in the first person is likely to sound irritatingly egotistical, you are more likely to write only a brief, informal, friendly foreword in the first person, sign it, then use the second person for the remainder of the booklet.

You have visualized your *audience* — that is, your readership. Before getting into organizing the material for the booklet, you'll do well at this point to visualize the *booklet* itself.

Make a rough dummy. If it's to be a 6″ x 9″ booklet of 16 pages plus separate cover, cut four 12″ x 9″ sheets of scratch paper and another 12″ x 9″ sheet of heavier paper. Put them together and fold through the center to make a 6″ x 9″ booklet. (Yes, there are 16 pages inside. Count them!) Now pin, or staple, or punch and tie the sheets together at the fold, and there is your rough dummy. Keep it before you. It will help you to see the booklet as a reality; help you to estimate more accurately the number of photographs and the amount of copy that can be used on those pages. In fact, as you work with the dummy, you'll find yourself *thinking* to fit the space allowed. More about working from a dummy is given later.

How Will You Organize Your Material?

Now the job begins to take shape! From here on it gets more exciting.

But just a minute. Stop and think again of that group of women to whom you are addressing the booklet, and of the objectives you hope to achieve.

BOOKLETS AS TEACHING AIDS

If you hope to have your booklets or leaflets used in schools, see page 88 for a discussion of what is acceptable.

DRAMATIZING LEAFLETS

In planning a leaflet, try to figure out some device that sets it apart. It may be a different way of boxing menus, or of handling fillers between recipes, or of using hand-written headings, etc. Some of your ideas will be discarded. But you can dream, can't you?

KNOW THE TERMS

In a conference about a forthcoming booklet or leaflet, the typographer or art director often speaks in terms of "picas," "letterpress," "offset," "20-lb. stock," etc. Best way to learn what such terms mean is to ask right then and there. Explanations take but a few seconds, are more likely to be remembered than information read in books.

BOOKLET PHOTOGRAPHS

Make sure that the photographs you use in a booklet are all the same tone. Spread them all out. If one looks lighter, weaker than the others, perhaps it can be printed with sharper contrasts, more punch. Avoid too great variety in backgrounds; the booklet will look smarter if there is some uniformity of background treatment. Consider bleeding the photos; that is, running them clear to the edges of the page. This often gives them more importance.

You want to interest as many of those women as possible in using your product in as many good ways as possible. That means, then, that from all the ideas you might conceivably use, you will select those you think will have the highest percentage of interest for those homemakers. They will be the ones which, if tried once, will be so well liked that they will be followed again and again. You will present those ideas in the booklet in a way that will attract interest and provoke action on the part of a high percentage of readers.

Undoubtedly by this time you have recognized that you can not possibly crowd into one booklet — even a 40-page one — all the good recipes and ideas you would like to use. Perhaps you started out thinking of a subject as general as "cookies." Soon you realized that it would take a large book to handle that subject adequately. So you have narrowed down your booklet to one sector of that big subject, and are thinking of "Cookies to Mail," or "Cookies Round the World," or "Holiday Cookies," or something of the sort.

When you have decided what seems to be the best possible choice and arrangement for subdivisions for your particular subject, set up a file folder for each one, labeling it properly. (For example, Rolled and Cut Cookies, Drop Cookies, Decorated Cookies, Bar Cookies, etc.) Now go through your files of tested and approved recipes, sort out the ones you think should be used, and drop them into the appropriate folders. Never do that selecting on the basis of "What do I have that I can put into this booklet?" Rather, keep thinking, "What will make this booklet of greatest help to the women who are to use it?"

Now make a list of the recipes in each folder. Count them. Estimate how much booklet space each one would require. Have you enough good ones to fill the pages? Study and analyze them. Are there too many of one type, not enough of another for good balance? Do the recipes selected play up the product as an important and necessary ingredient? Have you included those longtime and obvious favorites that your readers-to-be will look for in a booklet on cookies?

Read through those recipes again. Do they live up to the title of the booklet? Do they seem fresh and interesting as you read them over, or are they a bit stale and stodgy-sounding? Have you given new twists to the old favorites — worked out some improvements over the standard ways of making them, or figured out some tempting yet practical new ideas for serving or decorating them? If not, better get busy and bolster up the weak spots; fill in the holes. Make sure your booklet, brief though it may be, is complete as far as it goes.

See that the booklet has plenty of plus values, helpful tricks, and smart ideas worked in as asides; menus and notes to accompany some of the recipes. A booklet which shows this sort of thoughtful consideration for its readers is bound to have personality — the quality that sets it apart from the multitude of booklets, and gives it popularity — just as the girl who shows thoughtful consideration for her associates is bound to stand out in her crowd, bound to be popular.

Bringing a Booklet to Life

How a booklet is dramatized depends largely on the subject, and on the art director or artist with whom you are working. Most art directors, however, are interested in having the home economist's thoughts on how the various recipes and ideas might be illustrated or otherwise dramatized. It's good practice, too, to think them through from the artist's standpoint, and line up clippings illustrating your thoughts. If your ideas turn out to be impractical or unworkable or otherwise out of line from the artist's point of view, he will explain his reasoning, and you will have learned something more about planning booklets and leaflets.

TREND

Time was when educational bulletins were almost always written in third person impersonal style; were written about things rather than to persons. The trend now is to write directly to readers, using the "you" approach.

POINT OF VIEW

Most advertising booklets are written directly to the reader — that is, in the second person. Introductions to such booklets, however, are frequently written in the first person and signed by the home economist, using her trade name.

FINE POINTS IN
ANALYZING
After you have made your final selection of recipes, go over them once more. See if you have overused onions or garlic or tomato or some other item. If it's a booklet of main dishes, have you a good balance b e t w e e n top-of-range, broiler, and oven cookery? If it's a salad booklet, have you called for a wide variety of salad t y p e s and dressings? "Nothing in excess" is a good rule to remember.

MARGIN MEASURE

On a well-designed page, the inside, or gutter, margin is narrowest; the top margin slightly wider; outside margin w i d e r still; bottom margin widest of all.

TO ORGANIZE
MATERIAL

A cardboard carton isn't beautiful, but it does offer a convenient way of organizing material for a booklet. Get one a little wider than a file folder is long. Stand folders upright and go on from there. Such a box is easy to carry and to store. A neat file is, of course, better looking and more convenient.

If you are working under the guidance of an art director, by this time you will have been given a rough but definite layout of the booklet, either in dummy form, or spread by spread. If you are on your own, get out the rough dummy you made. Figure how you can dramatize it. Photographs, captions, headings, sub-heads, typography — all help dramatize a booklet. If it is not possible to use photographs or art work, then you must make the best possible use of words and type. Break up the pages! Break them up with menus; with boxes; with changes of type face — as shifting to italics or bold-face to emphasize a word or a line or paragraph.

Don't save your best pictures and recipes for the back pages of your booklet. Tests have shown over and over that a woman's enthusiasm — or lack of it — for a booklet is set almost instantaneously by the impression she gets from the first three or four pages. Switch your elements around so that you have something of sure-fire appeal in the beginning. It has much the same effect on readers as a hostess' smile of welcome has on her guests.

Mark off your dummy into your chosen subdivisions, apportioning more space to the more important or more appealing ones, less space to the others. Here is where your judgment, your sense of the significant, begin to show up.

Now spot your illustrations tentatively throughout these pages. You'll shift them around a dozen times, and make a dozen new dummies, probably, before you are through. Don't bunch photographs awkwardly; don't space them and place them exactly so many pages apart with deadly accuracy. Instead, work for a sense of rhythmic repeats throughout the booklet, with minor variations on the major theme.

So far, you are just playing with pictures and recipes, visualizing them roughly on the pages. At this stage you often will become aware of certain points, such as a recipe that seems extravagant or over-elaborate or otherwise out of line with other material in the booklet.

If you have been given an accurate sample page layout, and samples of the style and size of type to be used for each element of the page — i.e., recipe head, ingredients, body or method, chapter introduction, menu, filler, etc. — you are ready to figure the accurate character-count for each line, and the line-count for the page, and to fit your material to it. If you have no art director, ask the artist or printer or someone who understands such matters to advise you about these details. (See page 39, "Writing Copy To Fit Space.")

Before retyping your recipes to fit the character-count per line, it's a good idea to estimate the average number of *words* to each line, count the number of words in the body of each recipe, and get some idea as to how nearly those recipes are going to fit the space assigned for them. You may find you need to rewrite some of them, to shorten or lengthen them as the case may be. You may find you need to use fillers of a few lines here and there to make the pages come out right. However, it's well to consult the art director or artist before you do too much rewriting and juggling, for he may be delighted to utilize a bit of extra space for art work.

INSERTS

Packages of flour and other food products often carry recipe inserts. In planning those recipes, look at it this way: The woman has already bought the flour. Your job is to give her recipes that will tempt her to use that flour up fast and get another box or bag of it. Choose repeat recipes — ones she will want to make again and again.

How to "Weave" a Booklet Together

How you weave together the various ideas in each subdivision, the various subdivisions in the booklet, can make the difference between a flat, take-'em-or-leave-'em collection of suggestions, and a finished booklet, full of personality and appeal. You need an interesting theme that runs like a colorful cord throughout the entire booklet — through photographs, drawings, heads, introductions, captions, etc. — a cord that will tie the whole thing together into a neat package, and give the reader something to hold onto.

It is true that the theme of a booklet is largely a matter of art. But the writing and art must fit together, just as the words and music of a song go together. You write the words, you help the artist set the words to rhythm. Together you turn out a composition that will be a hit.

COMMENTS ON COVERS

If you want your booklet to have dignity and quality, keep the cover simple, with smart design, good lettering of title. Most artists prefer to avoid figure drawings on covers. When a white or very light cover stock is to be used, consider the advisability of an all-over design; it keeps the book cleaner looking.

How to Look at Your Booklet As a Whole

These sketches suggest two different systems for seeing a leaflet or booklet as a whole. Some writers prefer one; some another. To follow Layout *A*, simply take a sheet of ruled paper, draw a line down the center and number the lines as shown on diagram. Use as many lines as there are pages in your booklet. These numbered lines represent your pages. After the booklet is tentatively planned, fill out the outline, stating briefly what is on each page. Once those blanks are

		FRONT COVER
	INSIDE COVER	I INTRO
		2	3
A.		4	5
		6	7
		8	9
		10	11
		12	13
		14	15
		16	INSIDE BACK COVER
	BACK COVER	

PIN BEFORE YOU PASTE

Now you are ready to make up your booklet. Galleys of type are back from the printer, and all you have to do is trim them and paste them in the dummy. Before you begin pasting, however, better make up the entire booklet using pins to hold these bits and pieces of proof in place. If something does not come out right, it's easier to unpin than to unpaste!

filled, you can see at a glance how the copy balances; whether there is too much sameness, whether the theme is carried out rhythmically.

To follow the second system, (Layout *B*) draw little pages, spread by spread, as shown. Indicate photographs, recipes, menus, boxes, and the like.

With such a picture before you, you can see the pattern of the book as a whole, judge it as a unit. The important thing to remember is that a booklet must be a unified whole, not a hodge-podge of material. The more clearly you visualize that booklet as a unit, the more closely knit it will be when completed.

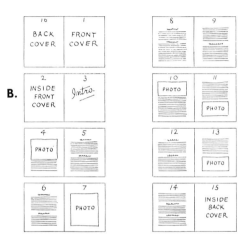

About Filing Booklets

One home economics director says, "When a booklet or a leaflet comes to my desk, I look it over carefully and mark on it the date it was received. Then on a small sheet of paper stapled to cover, I jot down notations as to specific recipes or ideas that might be useful in my particular job. The booklet is then ready for filing in one of the Princeton metal file boxes such as are used in libraries. (They are open at top and back so they can accommodate booklets of various sizes.) Each of these file boxes has a label on which are typed the titles of booklets filed therein. Once a year those files are checked. Booklets two years old or older are re-examined; some are kept, others discarded."

CONSIDER DISTRIBUTION

Are your booklets to be sent through the mail? Then consider the envelope along with the booklet. Remember, an envelope of odd size costs m o r e t o manufacture than a standard one. If you are planning a series of booklets, it's well to standardize the size and shape so that envelopes can be ordered in greater quantities at less expense. Also, the family of booklets may be filed together more neatly.

Are those leaflets to be distributed t h r o u g h stores? Better make them of a size that fits easily into a homemaker's purse.

SUGGESTIONS FOR PREPARING TEACHING MATERIALS*

ENCOURAGE *production and distribution of*:

1. Materials and visual aids which deal with situations that are familiar to students. (Example: Home kitchens, family situations.)

2. Written material which is well illustrated, balancing the amounts of space given to pictures and text.

3. Quality rather than quantity of materials. One excellent pamphlet is better than many less effective ones.

4. Posters sized in multiples of 8" x 11" to allow for folding and filing in standard-size file cabinets.

5. Material designed for different age groups. Keep materials easily readable, so that they can be used with more than one age or grade level.

6. Materials suitable for use with lower and middle income groups. All but a small percentage of our population come from these groups.

7. Materials that include sources of information and publication date.

DISCOURAGE *production and distribution of*:

1. Materials that produce anxiety or use fear for motivation.

2. Readymade lesson plans, quizzes, and tests. Good teachers prefer to plan with pupils and parents to meet needs in their home and community situations.

3. Historical material about a product or process. Very little time is spent in any modern home economics class on such study.

4. Materials that include steps in manufacturing or processing a product. This is information of minor importance in homemaking education, and teachers have little use for it.

5. Overdramatized material. This tends to distract attention from important facts, thereby lessening the value of the material as a teaching aid.

6. Samples for each pupil. These are a poor means of arousing interest, have little educational value, and their distribution is often prohibited by local school policy.

AVOID promotion of contests. Such methods of stimulating learning have serious disadvantages. They overemphasize competition and the importance of one person excelling another. They tend to encourage pupils to work primarily for prizes. They often create emotional tensions in pupils and teachers which interfere with learning.

*   *   *

* From *Business-Sponsored Home Economics Teaching Aids,* the published report of a national committee made up of home economists in business and education. (Out of print. Permission to reprint granted by Home Economics Education Branch, Office of Education, Department of Health, Education and Welfare, Washington 25, D.C.)

11.

Platform Demonstrations

The art of teaching
by showing how to do

NEVER UNDERESTIMATE the value of the demonstration and of the ability to give a good one. For the demonstration, carefully thought through and well presented, is a basic ingredient in home economics communications.

If you teach home economics at any level, practically every lesson is a demonstration. If you work in the equipment field, your job almost invariably includes showing homemakers how to use your range or refrigerator, your electric mixer or automatic washer.

If you are a "cupboard" home economist (i.e., a business home economist working with food items or household products) you may or may not be called upon to give platform demonstrations. But every time you prepare a set of directions to accompany a product, you do a show-how with words. If your food or household product is advertised on television, you are almost certain to work behind the scenes on concise, dramatized demonstrations for the commercials. If your department puts out a filmstrip or set of slides play-

Giving a demonstration is like tailoring a coat. The smallest detail is important.

ing up your product, almost every "frame" or picture is a demonstration detail.

As a home economics student or a beginning home economist, then, you need to learn all that you can about giving platform demonstrations. Once you've mastered the art, you can apply the principles in numerous ways.

Let's look at the steps to be taken in planning and doing demonstrations.

Consider Your Objective and Approach

In giving a demonstration of any type you have some specific message or lesson that you want to put across. Take salad making, for example.

When a home economics teacher gives a demonstration of making tossed green salads, her aim is simply to teach the fundamentals of making a basic tossed salad. If she were to give such a salad demonstration, live or on film, for an educational television station, her aim would be the same — to teach fundamentals. She would, however, need to put some special showmanship into it. And she might well work in some historical background to give greater depth and interest to her presentation.

When a business home economist employed by a manufacturer of salad oil or vinegar or seasonings gives a salad demonstration, she shows how to make a variety of new and interesting salads and dressings with her particular brand of ingredient. If the demonstration is to be for a TV commercial, she must ordinarily narrow down her presentation to just one salad at a time, and plan a quick, smooth show-how that will "sell" her salad ingredient to viewers.

A home economist in the equipment field may utilize salad-making ideas to interest homemakers in her make of refrigerator. Or she may use

A Mother-Daughter demonstration with a girl scout acting as helper to the home economist.

A Mr. and Mrs. feature, with a man and woman working together to get a complete meal.

A comparison of old and new methods of cake making: One w o m a n makes a cake by a standard method; the other whisks up a cake-mix cake. Comparison of time involved and amount of dishwashing re q u i r e d makes words unnecessary.

A buffet cart on which finished d i s h e s a r e placed, then w h e e l e d down the aisles for the audience to inspect.

the blender to whisk up new types of salad dressings. Or the range to make a glamorous new
cooked salad dressing.

And so it goes.

Until you know your objective and have defined your approach, you are certainly not ready
to plan the next step.

Visualize the Setup

Before you plan even the first step of a demonstration you need to have a picture of your audience, and of the physical setup for the presentation.

Is your audience to be a group of students or
of teachers? A gathering of young homemakers,
or a club of older, experienced women? Is it a
semisocial occasion, or a cooking school with any
and all types of persons attending — some just
for the door prizes, no doubt! What would your
audience probably be most interested in seeing
demonstrated? How much can those individuals
absorb in the way of skills? A demonstration
showing fancy tricks with bread dough might be
quickly grasped by a group of experienced homemakers. Younger ones may be equally interested,
but may need to have more of the demonstration
time given to the making of the yeast dough itself. The better you understand your audience,
the better focused will be your demonstration.

Now as to the setup. Will everyone in the audience be able to see what you are doing? What
about the stage? Is it well equipped, or must you
improvise, or alter the demonstration itself to
fit the physical setup? What about background?
What will you wear to harmonize with it? Will
the group be large or small? All these questions
enter into how you will plan and present your
show and your show-hows.

MORE THEMES

Wedding Gift Demonstra-
tion featuring small ap-
pliances.

After-Office Cooking, with
ideas for quick-fix meals.
Patio Cookery — with one
or two men getting into
the act.

How to Cook a Picture —
flash the picture on the
screen and then proceed
to show how to fix each
dish.

Party Fun From the
Freezer — a demonstra-
tion not of freezing, but
of using frozen foods of
all varieties.

TAPE IT

If feasible have a tape
recording made of your
demonstration. It will
help you to see and im-
prove possible weakness-
es. And it will be of help
if, later, your presenta-
tion is to be made into a
filmstrip or given on television.

Organize Your Plan of Work

If ever a job called for complete organization, a demonstration does.

Begin by figuring out exactly what you are going to do or make on the platform, and the order in which you will take every step.

Write down these steps in detail. Weigh them against the time allowed, the equipment available. It is assumed, of course, that you will not attempt to demonstrate a set of skills unless you have them in almost effortless perfection in your own fingers.

When the steps are established and you know that you can go through them without stumbling, study each step to determine what you are going to say about it. It is not enough to say flatly, "Rub the salad bowl with garlic."

You might explain that, used in this way, the garlic gives fragrance and flavor to the salad without overpowering it. Point out that you use a paper towel to brush out bits of garlic left after crushing. And, of course, admit that garlic can be omitted entirely, and perhaps a touch of herbs used in the salad instead.

Make your comments full, with reasons why. But keep in mind that when you have finished rubbing the bowl with garlic, you must be through talking about it. Timing is quite a trick, as every actor knows. It can make the difference between interest and boredom to audiences.

But it's not enough to organize your order of work and your line of talk. You must organize your marketing lists down to the last bunch of parsley; your equipment list down to the plastic bag for the washed lettuce; the list of jobs to be done in advance; the placing of each bowl and cup and tray on your work table. If you have an assistant, you and she must rehearse your parts so that as a team your movements are smooth, easy, and economical of time and steps.

If you are employed by a business concern with a well-developed home economics department, you may be given an entire presentation plan that has been worked out by someone else. If you are on your own, you will be responsible for every step of the organization plan. But regardless of who does that planning, you must have the entire picture in your mind as well as on paper before you get up on the platform. And it must be as attractive, interesting, and dramatic a picture as you can make it.

Dramatize Your Demonstration

When you stand before your home economics class or group of homemakers you are, in a sense, a showman. As such, you need to dramatize your demonstration — bring it to life — in every way that you can, yet not detract from the points you are trying to put across. Here are things to do:

Give your demonstration an appealing title. Get news into your show. Maybe you have a new product, or a new feature added to an established product. Certainly you can show new uses for a well-known product or piece of equipment; new recipes, new ways of serving and garnishing a familiar food.

Put originality into the wording of the title, as did the home economist who called her laundering demonstration a "soap opera." But never be content to parrot the phrases of others. Shake your own idea tree, and you can surely come up with a fresh and fresh-sounding title that is just right.

Get off to a dramatic start. If you are going to show how to decorate cakes, bring on a beautiful wedding cake or birthday cake at the beginning of the demonstration. Show it off with pride. Then go on to say (in effect), "This is a preview

COLOR COUNTS

The platform with its bright lights and shining equipment is trying on the eyes. Bring in color and pattern wherever you can, even to those red tomatoes and peppers to be seen when you open the refrigerator door. Gay dishcloths, pot holders, aprons, dishes, all help to bring life to the setting. If possible, keep the curtain drawn until time for the show to begin

of one of the things we are going to do today. Now let's start from the beginning, and see how easy it is, and how much fun it is, to decorate a beautiful cake."

Figure out how to get the effect of camera "close-ups." A platform demonstration, for most of the audience, consists of "long shots" or "intermediate shots" in television language. An overhead mirror can be mighty helpful in showing a process or a finished dish, but it is not the complete solution.

In order to focus sharply on what you are showing or doing, keep your working space free of clutter and confusion. Avoid "busy" designs in backgrounds or china, dress or apron. In general use soft grayed colors in china in order to show up foods to best effect — but don't forget to use some touches of red to give life to your display!

Remember that fairly large items are much easier to see than little tiny things. If you wish to show something small, such as fancy-shaped little rolls, perhaps you can make up one roll several times larger than normal in order to show just how you proceed. Remember that the audience has come to see what you are doing, not just to listen to what you say you are doing.

Use meaningful household words as you talk. If you say "sauté" or some other word that may not be in the vocabularies of those in the audience, define it. Better yet, use other simple words to express what sauté means. ("Cook the chopped onions in the oil in a skillet," or "Brown the cubes of beef quickly in a little melted shortening in a frying pan," or the like.) Never be guilty of using trite, worn-out phrases and dated slang. Work in plenty of human-interest stories or incidents rather than "funny" stories learned for the occasion. Mentioning how you used to have to tiptoe across the room when your mother made an angel food cake will send friendly nods of under-

COOKING SCHOOL RECOMMENDATIONS

1. Strive for helpfulness.

2. Use familiar, tested recipes.

3. Be sure of yourself.

4. Be patient. Take time to answer questions, but keep the question-asking under control.

5. Always repeat the question your are answering.

6. Be sincere and tactful. Suggest rather than dictate.

7. Be friendly. Look friendly.

8. Keep the audience with you.

9. Summarize what you have done.

10. Give them something to remember you by, such as a set of recipe cards or a leaflet that tells in type what was done on the platform.

standing through an audience of older women; will mean little to young women who have known nothing but standardized recipes and mixes, and regulated ovens.

Handle heavy information with a light touch. Forget that pompous lecturing tone of voice, and visit with the audience in a friendly me-to-you way. Yes, you can do it and still keep your position of authority. Put a little fun into the session. Laugh at yourself if you make a slight mistake. Never be self-consciously apologetic.

Encourage audience participation. Allow time for questions. Call for a show of hands occasionally, or ask the audience to clap for favorite dishes. If it seems sensible, invite one of the women to the platform to wash her hands and roll out the pastry or turn out a gelatin mold according to your directions. (Some pre-arrangement is advisable here, perhaps.)

Display the finished products in some interesting way so that the audience will carry home clear mental pictures of them.

In your search for the dramatic, however, keep in mind that a demonstration is to show how, not to show off. Don't attempt more in any session than you can do well, or more than the audience can absorb. Try a few spectacular stunts, if you like, such as sliding a baked custard pie filling into a baked pie shell. But, for the most part, keep to skills that women in the audience will use again and again in their own kitchens.

Give them something to remember you by. Be sure to have recipes or other printed information ready so that everyone present has something to take away with her. Discuss these with the audience. Sell homemakers on wanting the material. Don't say, "There are some recipes there on the table if you want them" — or words to that effect! Whether you do or do not give out take-homes, do give everyone in the audience a fresh word or

The successful demonstrator has vitality and enthusiasm — enough of both to carry over into the audience.

HOW MANY DISHES

One home economist says: "In giving a foods demonstration, figure to make not more than 6 or 7 dishes in a 1-hour show; not more than 9 in a demonstration lasting 1½ hours."

WHEN YOU DEMONSTRATE EQUIPMENT

It is not enough merely to introduce a piece of equipment. It must be discussed and described so that every woman in the audience becomes acquainted with it. Danger lies in too much talk-talk about the fine points of the range or sewing machine—not enough translating into uses; not enough show-how. Here's where you need to dramatize by means of meaningful words.

Remember, *you* are familiar with that piece of equipment, familiar with the terms used by the manufacturer. Give the audience time to absorb those details.

thought and a reassuring friendly smile to carry away with her.

And above all else, be sincere. If you approach your demonstration from the standpoint of really wanting to help and inspire your audience, you will feel some of that same inspiration yourself. With it, you are sure to put your demonstration across in a way that will please everyone concerned with it.

Authors' Note: There is far more to this subject than is suggested by this chapter. But demonstration techniques are learned by doing, not by reading. Every home economist who gives a finished performance has learned her art the hard way — by doing and doing and doing, or by working under the direction of someone whose techniques and synchronization are perfect. Analyze every demonstration that you see; ask yourself what makes it good or not so good. Analyze your own demonstrations; figure how each one might be improved in subject matter, or speeded up, or worked out more smoothly. A demonstration moves along step by step. It is only by improving *yourself* step by step that you learn to do a finished job.

12.

Educational Films and Slides

Pointers on planning
and producing them

In the first edition of this book (1949), more attention and more pages were devoted to educational slides and motion picture films as teaching aids than to filmstrips. Since then, the filmstrip has become increasingly important. And more and more business home economists find themselves working on the preparation of this type of visual aid.

Homemaking supervisors and teachers appreciate a good filmstrip for several reasons. Since the film consists of a series of close-up photographs ("frames") which are enlarged on the screen, everyone in the classroom can see each operation as if she were standing at the teacher's elbow. And since the pictures are "stills" there is time for everyone to observe details that might be lost in a platform demonstration or a movie film presentation.

A lot of action and information can be telescoped into small space and short time. More ground can be covered effectively in a 20-minute filmstrip than in a 40-minute "live" demonstra-

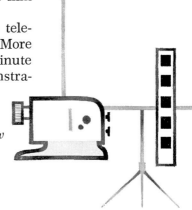

The filmstrip spotlights practical homemaking information, setting it aglow with life and color.

tion. Sharply focused, the filmstrip can omit non-essentials, emphasize essentials . . . bright with color and light, it gives a touch of excitement to unexciting subjects . . . simple to transport and to show, it can be worked into a school homemaking program at the most suitable and convenient time . . . and — highly important from the education standpoint — it can be previewed before being shown to classes, in order to make sure that desirable techniques are demonstrated.

Where Do You Begin?

When you, a business home economist, are first confronted with the responsibility of planning and producing a filmstrip, the assignment seems formidable. But when you realize that it is after all a matter of presenting a demonstration in pictures rather than in person, you're ready to go to work.

If you haven't been assigned a specific subject in advance, you will probably proceed somewhat in this order.

Since this is to be a teaching aid — or, rather, a learning aid — you ask yourself, "What would homemaking teachers and supervisors like to have their students learn about using the product that I am concerned with?"

You jot down several possible subjects that could be presented in pictorial lessons. Some of these you realize are too broad in scope to cover adequately within the limitations of 40 or so frames and 18 to 20 minutes running time that is recommended. ("Salads," for example, would be entirely too inclusive; but "Bowl Salads" or "Molded Salads" would be quite possible. "Making a Dress" would probably be too broad as a subject for a filmstrip — but "Buttons and Buttonholes" might make sense.)

LENGTH

To make the showing of an educational filmstrip really educational, it must be introduced by the teacher, and the showing must be followed by discussion to clinch the points made. To fit all this into a 40 to 50 minute class period, running time for the filmstrip itself should not exceed 18 to 20 minutes.

CAPTIONS

In some filmstrips each photograph (i.e., frame) has a brief caption lettered on it, which helps the students get the point of the picture clearly and quickly. Such captions must fit the space allowed, and still say something!

The filmstrip does lack one advantage that a good platform demonstration has — the personality and enthusiasm of the "live" home economist. This lack must be made up for in the quality of the pictures and the wording, and in the enthusiasm of the teacher presenting the film.

Even while you are considering subjects and titles, you are mentally running through the possible steps that should be shown under each one, and estimating how many frames would be needed.

Having come to some conclusions and outlined them on paper, you discuss them with your own executive director. (Isn't it amazing what good ideas and judgment men have about homemaking subjects?) Then you are ready to ask a few representative homemaking supervisors and teachers in your territory if they will give you their frank opinions on your tentative plans.

Guided and fortified by the generous suggestions of your consultants, you are ready to work out a more definite and detailed outline of the projected filmstrip. You decide on the subheads that belong under your general title. Under each of these you list the series of steps which you feel should be given and can be pictured under each subhead. While you are visualizing those pictured steps, and the occasional glamour display shots that may be called for, you'll be wise to "rough out" tentative captions for them, and make notes of points that should be covered in words in the accompanying voice commentary.

You have to do all of these more or less simultaneously, weighing, juggling, mentally struggling, until finally everything falls into an orderly and logical arrangement. And, to your amazement, you'll find you come out with just about the right number of frames! Now more conferring will probably be in order, to make sure that you are still on the right track.

Once the job is defined and the action steps visualized and organized, the hardest part of the work is actually done. True, there still remains that small matter of setting up 40 or more photographs. But it is a concrete job to do, and if you have had any experience in photography you

SHOW OF HANDS

Most filmstrips are smoother if only hands, rather than full-figure models are used. Hand pictures can be shot faster, make better close-ups, and are less distracting to the viewers. A filmstrip for use at high school level should feature young-looking hands.

know how to approach it. If you haven't, an experienced home economics consultant will probably be called in to work with you.

Sketch Out Those "Frames"

ON WRITING SKITS AND SCRIPTS

In both, the big thing is to get across one central idea, play up one central character. First decide what these are to be, then build your story step by step. Work it out simply and directly, keeping the central idea always in mind. *See* those steps as pictures. When you learn to *think* pictorially you can *write* pictorially!

You will probably find it helpful and time-saving if you make a rough sketch of just what is to be shown in each frame. Suggest the action. List supplies, utensils, and other props that may be needed. Note what colors are to be featured in each sequence. Figure how to heighten and brighten the color impact.

A conference with the photographer at this stage will help settle such problems as best order of shooting, choice of model, table tops and wall backgrounds, etc. He will show you just what the working space — the photographic field — will be. (Incidentally, since he will be working on a budget of both time and money, it may be necessary to plan to do 10 or more setups a day.)

When it comes to actual shooting, avoid showing the package or trade name of your product too obtrusively or too often. Omit confused backgrounds and extra accessories. Get the camera right down into the action. Let the hands tell the story. Think twice before showing more than hands — faces and figures tend to distract. Avoid apron designs that carry the eyes of the viewer away from the action. Keep the pictures clean and "lean."

When the photographing has been completed, forget it for a day or two. By the time the photographer has a finished set of slides to show you, you will be ready to appraise them. Now your work narrows down into writing the captions and commentary. Yes, you will probably have written preliminary copy for both, but more writing and rewriting will be necessary to put the important points across in the space allowed.

If it has been decided that titles and captions will be lettered on the frames, a skilled typographer will be called on to set the words in type so that they can be transferred to the slides. But first *you* have to write those words! That requires arithmetic as well as writing. You'll be given a sample of type showing the exact character count (letter count) for those words in the one or two lines of caption space allowed — and you must write to fit that space.

Eventually — if not sooner — you must do the finished commentary. This may be handled vocally on a sound track; or it may be printed, for the teacher to read aloud as she operates the projector. In either case, the comment on each frame should be brief. If the remarks accompanying one frame run long (that is, much over 30 seconds), an extra frame should probably have been included.

Here again it's well to get the advice of your teacher-consultants before the commentary is printed or recorded. You will want to get their views, too, about the material to be distributed to the students.

Educational Motion Pictures

Although many educational motion pictures based on homemaking material are used on television and in classrooms, most of them are written and produced by film companies. Whatever the home economist does is done under the direction of the producer. Aside from utilizing her technical skills, she has few responsibilities other than to follow orders, to make suggestions when they are pertinent to the success of the picture, and to cooperate in every way possible.

When and if you, a home economist, are involved in planning, writing, and following through on a motion picture, a good rule to fol-

FILM FOLLOW-UPS

Most educational films and slides need a follow-up — something tangible that students can see or read or use after the film is finished. That follow-up can be in the form of posters, charts, displays, leaflets, or booklets. In the commercial home economics film, material of that sort is prepared by the business home economist. If such a task falls to you, make that follow-up a clincher or condensation of the central theme of the film. But make it a unit in itself, so that it is usable with or without the accompanying film.

FILMSTRIP COMMENTARY

The teachers' commentary illustrated here is a 12-page folder, done in notebook size (8½" x 11"). On cover of folder (see layout sketch) space has been allowed to set forth aims of filmstrip. On subsequent pages each frame is reproduced with a paragraph of discussion for the teacher to read aloud while that frame is being shown. Note that some paragraphs are quite brief, others longer — but none run longer than 70 words. (Reproduced by permission of C and H Sugar Corporation.)

low is to keep plot, plan, and pictures as simple as possible.

Looking To the Future

What will be the future of educational filmstrips? Will those to be used in television call for new techniques? How about preparing such visuals for use in foreign countries where home economics is just being established? Will the time come when a homemaker can take out filmstrips from the public library just as she now takes out books? Will supermarket home economists use filmstrips to show shoppers how to use new household products?

Do not tune in five years from now to see what has happened. Instead, tune into tomorrow right now! Project your own thinking into the future, and have a part in its making.

13.

Television and Radio Scripts

How to write for
airwave audiences

WITH THE EXCEPTION of this chapter, all of the statements in this book are based on the first-hand knowledge and experiences of the authors. These notes on television represent the composite thinking of men and women (in various parts of the country) who are actively engaged in producing, or helping to produce, television programs of interest to homemakers and future homemakers.

In considering their recommendations, it's well to keep in mind that much of what is said about television today may or may not apply tomorrow. This is true, of course, of all types of communications, but doubly so of television and radio — both of which are relatively new in the world of words.

Whatever changes are wrought, three basic facts will always apply:

1. The strength of a television program depends directly on the *vision* of those who conceive and produce it.

2. The word "television" suggests that there should be something visual to interpret what is

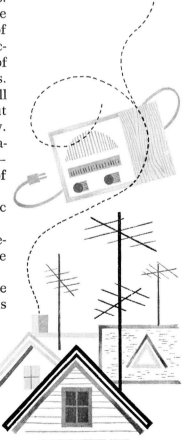

Educational television is the home economist's opportunity to get on the same wave length as the homemakers.

being said. Except, perhaps, in instances where something of wide interest is reported by persons of strong personal appeal, such interpretive visuals are not only an adjunct but a necessity. Even in newscasts they are used freely, to bring words and events to life, to fill in background, and to provide variety and thus hold attention.

3. The great factor in television is timing. Unless the program gets off to a good start immediately and sustains interest to the end, it will not be followed. For that reason, thinking must forever start with, "What is the idea I want to put across?" In other words, what is my "topic sentence?"

The Television Commercial

FACT TO FACE

Television w r i t i n g is thinking in terms of pictures. To some persons the ability to think pictorially comes naturally; for others it is hard to do. It is something each person must develop within herself.

Shortest of all television presentations is the commercial or spot announcement. In one minute or less a product or an idea must be presented and put into motion in a way that prompts the viewer to action. In a commercial, that desired action is to buy and use a specific product.

Where does the home economist fit into planning and producing television commercials? What does the beginning home economist need to develop if she is to fit successfully into that picture?

According to a number of business home economists, good technical skills plus experience in working with photographers are of prime importance. Because of the high cost of producing a commercial, either live or taped, many minds must work together to figure out exactly what is to be shown and what is to be said about it. The firm's advertising agency usually carries most of the responsibility for planning and producing commercials. The home economist may or may not be included in the preliminary "brain-storming."

However, once the idea has been decided upon, her knowledge and skills will be needed. If it is a food product, she will make up the featured dish not once but several times for all to study. Various changes and improvements will be suggested before the subject is considered ready to go. Every detail of that salad or casserole or dessert will be considered thoughtfully — the type of salad bowl or plate and how the hands will pour the dressing; the surface detail and degree of brownness of the casserole; the texture and swirl of the pie filling.

Whether the commercial is to be taped or shown live, the general procedure is much the same. A series of still pictures will probably be made, illustrating each step that will be shown on TV. With these in hand, the timing of the announcer's script to fit the action can be worked out. Also, if need for further improvement should show up in these photographs, changes can be made before the commercial appears on home screens.

Frequently the show for which such commercials are designed goes on the air "live," in a city far from the home economist's home base. In such case, the approved recipe and photographs may be turned over to a home economics consultant in that area. If her hands are photogenic (as well as graceful and steady) they may be used in the action and display shots as well as for doing the background preparation. If not, a professional model's hands will be used, and the home economist will work with her behind the scenes as necessary.

Sometimes the consultant is bypassed, and the professional model proceeds according to the photographs. This means that the home economist who works on the original pictures must be extra careful to visualize each step completely, anticipating possible awkwardness on the part

QUESTION

By cooperating with the producers of children's programs, might it not be possible to stimulate an interest in homemaking in very small children? In a song-and-dance show, for one example, include hippety-hopping to the market and tip-toeing from shelf to shelf. By watching children's shows on educational channels, ideas along this line will suggest themselves.

of a non-home economist model. Just how is she to "dot" that casserole with butter? How serve the crumb crust pie successfully, or top that pudding with whipped-cream-from-a-can? The more the young home economist learns to think in pictures, the more valuable she will be in every phase of TV productions, including the commercial.

The Four-Minute Short

Many half hours on the air are made up of four- to five-minute shorts, with announcements or commercials sandwiched in between.

What is the basic problem in planning and doing such shorts? Successful producers of women's interest programs stress the importance of high-appeal subject matter, narrowed down to some one idea that can be telescoped into those few minutes. Obviously, this means presenting only one segment of a broad subject. The care of clothing, for example (one aspect of the still broader subject of money management), would have to be reduced to one category of clothing, such as shoes, hats, sweaters, or handbags — each a specific subject for a four-minute presentation.

Here again, program planners interviewed mention the need for some sort of visual in every television short — and the simpler, the better. As one programmer says, "Four minutes may seem to be a relatively short period of time, but it is too long to look at one face unless there is something interesting going on."

That brief talk on shoe care is strengthened when actual shoes in varying stages of wear and/ or repair are displayed and talked about. A discussion of any phase of nutrition calls for charts or — better — displays of actual foods. A presentation on home lighting needs proper lamps or

FINE POINTS

Keep in mind the value of the dramatic pause; the value of the understatement vs. the exaggerated build-up; the value of the light touch vs. heavy-handed plugging.

photographs of lamps to bring the subject matter to life. In other words, something to look at!

What about those photographs that are to be displayed in television? The director of one business organization whose television releases are popular with dozens of stations and programmers has this to say about them:

1. Work for photographic simplicity — the simplest of accessories and as few of them as possible. Get across just one idea in every picture.

2. Pose such photographs as horizontals, so that they are in proportion to the home screen.

3. Watch the lighting. Make sure there are no shadows that will look like holes when the photograph is shown. If shadows are apparent when the photographs are being made, move in additional lighting or move the lights around in order to kill those shadowy areas. Work for contrast, but avoid sharp blacks and dead whites, both of which come out as mere blanks on the home television screen.

4. Unless you know that a specific programmer prefers glossy prints, have all photographs done in nonglossy finish. Most stations prefer these.

5. Using paper cutter, trim off white borders from all prints. If it seems advisable to crop a picture, do so, but keep to the proportions of the 8″ x 10″ picture.

6. Mount every photograph on heavy mat board (gray or color) to provide a frame for the picture and to keep it from buckling or bending when displayed. (A card 11″ x 14″ is right for an 8″ x 10″ photograph from which white border has been removed.) The director who generously gave the foregoing recommendations uses colored mat board for mounting photographs. Shown in black and white television, the color comes through in gray. Shown on color TV, they add a lively touch to black-and-white photographs.

LEARN FROM SCIENCE PROGRAMS

Note that in most televised science presentations, only *one* basic fact is taught or brought out at a time. Whatever the science subject, it is reduced to simple language, is made informal, informative, entertaining, and completely understandable. The same can apply in "domestic" science programs!

TEACHING VIA TV

Surveys show that students like to see other students perform in televised lesson presentations; that they respond to activity rather than to lecturing; that they derive more value from a program viewed in the classroom than when seen in the auditorium with other groups participating.

The Interview, Joint Conversation, Panel Discussion

When a program runs for 13 minutes or longer, two or more persons often make for a more interesting presentation than when only one person gets into the act. In any twosome, the interviewer logically takes the lead and asks the questions. In a group discussion, the master of ceremonies (man or woman) poses the question or problem, and designates the person who is to discuss it. The more the interviewer or M.C. keeps to that position, the stronger the show — provided, of course, the one being interviewed or questioned has something worthwhile to say and knows how to say it! The one in charge must be ever on the alert to move in if the subject matter gets out of hand or bogs down. And every person in a two-way or group discussion must know in advance exactly what is to be discussed and at what length. When the panel discussion or interview is used in teaching-by-television, the teacher actually and rightly leads, even though a student or young adult may appear to do so.

VOICE CULTURE

Whether on television or radio, the voice is important. One program director urges the home economist to d e v e l o p three voice qualities — friendliness, authority, and enthusiasm. Also, to pitch her voice low.

The Televised Lesson Plan

At the time this is being written, teaching via television is still in the experimental stage — and it always will be! No two teachers will ever proceed in exactly the same way. No two groups of students will respond in exactly the same manner. No set of rules can be given that will apply to all types of subject matter and all types of groups. Here, however, are ten recommendations from an ex-teacher, based on years of classroom work and months of viewing.

1. Work for variety within a pattern of continuity. That is, stick to one type of approach throughout the series, but introduce plenty of surprise features. Identify your program by carrying some one type of visual — as chalk

board or paper dolls — through the series; in other words, establish a "trade-mark" for your show.

2. Give plenty of reasons why. In a televised lesson there is no opportunity for students to ask questions. Hence the need to anticipate them.

3. Be content to establish one point in each lesson. Too much information, too many facts, too many ideas at a time are difficult to absorb.

4. Keep at an easy pace — not too fast, not too slow. Explain the meaning of words that may not be in the students' vocabularies.

5. Try to have a depth interview with a student at the end of the program. Group evaluation is valuable, but may not bring out as much specific information as when one student is interviewed at length and alone.

6. Watch your taped show occasionally with a group of students. Study not only what comes through on the screen, but study the students as they watch.

7. Extend the thinking scope of students and other viewers by posing an occasional problem that each must reason out to his own satisfaction.

8. Enrich the television lesson by tying in with history, geography ,travel, art, and other subjects that may have a bearing on what is presented. In such ways, students' minds are led out beyond the narrow boundaries of provincial thinking. (And that, of course, is the basic meaning of the word "educate" — to lead out.)

9. Be enthusiastic about the subject matter and those you hope to interest. Teaching — whether in the classroom or over the air — must be dynamic if it is to accomplish its end.

10. Try to be relaxed. No, on second thought, *don't try!* If you are truly enthusiastic about and full of your subject, and eager to communicate that interest and enthusiasm to your students, you will not be selfconscious!

YOU'RE ON THE AIR

Before you go on, hum, note by note, up and down the scale. When you strike your lowest natural note, talk. That is likely to be a good place to pitch your voice for the broadcast. Stand or sit comfortably. Take a deep breath. Relax. Talk directly to some one person that you know is listening. And don't hurry.

PROGRAM OUTLINE
(Basic)

Name:
Date:
Subject:
Names of Participants:

Properties: (what you will bring)
(what you want station to furnish)

Objective: (What you are trying to accomplish)

Time Estimate	Say	Show
	Introduction List the sequence of ideas that you want to put across. These can be in questions that you intend to answer. Plan general amount of time you will spend on each point you will be making. Summarize the main points you make as you go along. **Ending** Save some of the less important things till the end so that you can either cut or stretch easily depending on the time you have left. Include the main ideas you want viewers to remember.	List the order in which you will use the visuals. This order is very important for the director in order to get the camera set up for the right shots.

NOTE: This program outline was developed by Ardis W. McMechan, assistant extension editor (home economics television), Iowa State University through working with a number of television stations and nonprofessional television performers as one of the easiest ways for them to work with one another. Similar types of run-down sheets are used by stations in general. Keep your outline limited to *one* page and make it an outline — not a word for word script.   R/C

PROGRAM OUTLINE
(Specific Examples)

Name: Sally Home Economist
Date: June 10, Wednesday
Subject: Sewing on new fabrics
Names of participants:
        self

Properties: I will bring a sewing machine and examples of man-made fibers and blends with natural fibers. Will need a table to work on.

Objective: To point out the sewing machine adjustments necessary in sewing synthetic fabrics.

Time Estimate	Say	Show
1 min.	Beautiful new fabrics made from synthetic fibers or blends with natural fibers now ready for spring sewing. Have some tips ready to pass along to make your sewing most successful.	Show examples of fabrics.
3 min.	Why is stiching synthetics different from natural fibers? Discuss difference between single filament and staple yarns.	Point out trouble spots on sewing machine. Use all dacron for specific example.
2 min.	Point out importance of avoiding stitching with the lengthwise grain.	CU on small sample of stitchery on synthetic fabrics.

4 min.	What adjustments are necessary on the machine for stitching?
	   1. top tension
	   2. pressure foot adjustment
	   3. needle hole and needle
		Demonstrate making these adjustments on the machine.

2 min.	Discuss other points in sewing on the various types of synthetic fabrics.	Show other examples of fabrics.
1 min.	Close: Remember it does take these special sewing machine adjustments to sew synthetic fabrics. If you learn these adjustments you'll enjoy using these kinds of fabrics more.	Point out on sewing machine.

When You Face That Camera

Whenever you appear in a television program, remember these personal rules:

Wear well-fitting clothes in pastel tones, with sleeves of becoming length. (Extremely short sleeves make arms look awkward.) Avoid bizarre prints and bold designs in clothing. Beware of glittery jewelry. Make sure the hair is becomingly done — and not too recently. Tight curls or waves are inclined to look hard and artificial.

Talk quietly, distinctly, informally, and sincerely. Many a televised demonstration, perfect in every other detail, leaves listeners cold because the demonstrator never smiles. Look directly into the camera from time to time. Don't talk to that sewing machine needle or into that bowl! Avoid rustling or crumpling paper, clinking metal. Use wooden spoons and rubber scrapers, and, for some purposes, plastic bowls, to cut down noise. Make sure that visuals employed are sharply clear, but free from "bounceback" of light or reflections. Keep action to a small area. Do not move around more than is necessary. When you must move, do so slowly. Whether you do an actual show-how (demonstration) or use visuals as a conversation piece, practice so that you use your hands skillfully and with grace and ease.

INTERVIEWED

When asked for an opinion, think through your answer before you give it. Remember, you are going to be quoted. Don't talk too much; let the interviewer guide the conversation. If there is something that might make for confusion, write out your statement, so that the interviewer will have your exact wording.

What About The Future?

Probably no two persons agree completely as to the future — or even the present — of television. Many educators believe that teaching via television offers far greater opportunities than have been developed to date. Many are urging programs designed to teach homemaking skills to very young children — the ones who are most enthusiastic about learning such exciting things! Most are convinced that since every television presentation is an experiment, it should be taped for evaluation afterward. All must admit that television of the future will depend on the vision of those who are concerned with it. Suggested motto: *Without vision, television must perish.*

No two persons seem to agree as to the state and status of homemaking programs sponsored by advertising. One observer reports, "We have no homemaking programs in our community." Another says, "In our city we have three commercially sponsored women's interest programs, plus two on our local educational station."

As to subject matter, some directors recognize the appeal of fashions and clothing, reject programs on cooking, housekeeping, and cleaning because, they say, to women viewers these subjects represent tiresome work. Some of us would go further, and admit that *watching* certain programs of that type could be classified as tiresome work! But surely ways can be devised to make them interesting and important enough to watch.

Whatever one's individual opinion — whether as planner, producer, or viewer — one fact stands out: The home economist's opportunity in television is what she makes it.

What About Radio?

Like television, radio is changing. New stations are being built; more will be. Programs (some of them, at least) are improving. While at this writing there are relatively few radio programs that deal exclusively with homemaking information, that may not be true by the time this book is published. New thinking is being done. New ideas will be tried out. Here, again, the future, so far as home economists are concerned, will depend on the ideas of those home economists who aspire to this form of communication. Meanwhile, here are six points to keep in mind:

RADIOGRAMS

Radio is personal journalism — it must have that special me-to-you quality . . . There's no use writing conversation, unless it's broadcast in a conversational manner. . . Don't use a lot of figures — listeners won't remember them. . . Have an extra paragraph or two at the end of the script that can be used or not, depending on the time.

1. Radio script must be written for the ear, not for the eye. You must learn to talk on paper.

2. Radio is personal journalism, which means it needs to have that me-to-you feeling in it. You must talk not as you would to a large audience, but as you would to one friend in her own home. This feeling of intimacy and understanding is especially important in the home economics radio or television program. But underlying your friendly informality must be a feeling of genuine authority on the subject under discussion.

3. Radio calls for plenty of word pictures. You must make your listeners see things as you describe them. If you are talking about a lemon meringue pie, help each woman to see that pie with its high meringue tinged with golden brown; taste its tart-sweet filling; mentally bite into its tender-crisp crust. Help her to visualize herself making that pie step by step.

"We need imagination in programming not sterility; creatively, not imitation; experimention, not conformity; excell e n c e, not mediocrity." — Newton N. Minow

4. Radio needs simple words, short and simple sentences. That means no long, detailed recipes or directions; no foreign cooking terms. "Don't broadcast a recipe calling for more than six ingredients" is a rule that many experienced home commentators follow.

5. Radio calls for careful timing. If you are giving a recipe over the air, you must speak slowly so that listeners can write down what you are saying. One good way to manage this timing is to write the recipe yourself as you give it.

6. Radio demands above all else that a program sound sincere. That means it must *be* sincere. Sincerity is something you cannot fake. It's something you must feel inside yourself. You can get away with some voice weaknesses, if your helpful spirit and real knowledge shine through between your lines. In other words, if you have something really worth saying, and if you think of your audience while you are saying it, chances are your time on the air will be time well invested for your listeners.

14.

Magazine Writing

What are the
facts today?

HAVE YOU HAD a secret ambition to work on or for a home-centered magazine — perhaps not at present, but at some time in the future? Have you wondered what qualifications you would need, what talents you might develop, and how you might best approach an editor to sell yourself and your ideas?

Unfortunately there are no specific answers to that last question. If you analyze the problem thoughtfully, however, you will emerge with some such reasoning as this:

Every magazine — particularly a magazine designed to appeal to homemakers — is put together by a staff of specialists to interest some specific group of readers. Therefore, if you hope to become a staff editor or an outside contributor, you, too, must be a specialist. That is the place to start your thinking.

Now make a study of homemaking publications. Try to figure out the type of homemakers to which each publication hopes to appeal. Observe the mastheads of those magazines. Note the

Magazine writing, like good family relations, is built on understanding. Before you attempt it, you must know the magazine's needs.

[115]

WHAT ABOUT PHOTOGRAPHS?

In general, it's advisable not to invest money in commercial photographs unless you are reasonably sure that an editor is interested in your material. It is, however, sometimes good sense to send along a snapshot to show the editor exactly what your idea is about. If you are redoing some part of your home and hope to write a story about it later, do have "before" pictures made; then when the remodeling is completed, have the same photographer do "after" shots from exactly the same angle.

FOR THE WRITE-MINDED

If you want to write for magazines, look into the dozens of trade and industrial and religious and travel and local and other special-interest magazines which publish s o m e material on homemaking. Study their editorial and advertising columns before submitting y o u r manuscript.

How do you locate samples of such publications? By asking questions; by checking at the library; by keeping your eyes open; by following magazines that list potential markets for all types of articles.

long list of editors, contributing editors, and editorial assistants. Realize that some of these editors specialize in subject matter, as foods or equipment; others in art or photography or copy editing. Among the persons listed may be one or more who were hired because of their ability to produce new ideas, or to do a skillful job of interviewing.

The question now becomes how to fit you and/or your writing into that existing picture.

Let's say that you have a sound background in foods, and rightfully, consider yourself a food specialist. That's good, but it is no indication that what you write about foods will be published. Remember, the magazine you plan to approach already has a staff of qualified food editors.

"But," you may say, "I've specialized in foreign cookery." That's something of a specialty, but it may not be enough to interest an editor who probably receives a number of articles on foreign cookery during the year. If, however, you have narrowed down your study to short-cut American adaptations of foreign cookery, you may have a specialty that could conceivably appeal to the food editor of a home magazine.

In writing that editor — and you should always query an editor before submitting an article of any length — tell her briefly about your narrowed-down specialty. Describe in part your idea for an "Instant Smorgasbord"; your Americanized version of sukiyaki in which slices of Monterey Jack cheese are used in place of the traditional bean curd. Mention your recipe for Easy Way Chinese Fortune Cookies, and one or two other examples of the 15 or 20 recipes you have developed. State, finally, that you are a graduate home economist and have thoroughly tested your material.

Even though you have developed what you feel is a good, fresh idea, and even though you have written a good letter of query to the editor, you may find that the editor is not interested, or that she is not able to use such an article due to the limits of space. But you will have proceeded in the professional way and can go on from there to approach another editor, or to reshape your idea, or to conceive another one.

Another Way to Specialize

Many free-lance writers specialize in digging out fresh ideas and reporting on them. Here's how it can apply to you.

You are, let's say, a stay-at-home homemaker with a home economics degree. Your major may have been family relations, child development, or whatever. But now you are married, living in a tract area of new homes, and interested in observing how various families have solved some specific problem, such as expanding storage areas. By keeping your eyes open, you learn that one family has built a ventilated floor-to-ceiling closet into one corner of the porch to make a storage place for rain-gear. You find a kitchen-minded homemaker who has rebuilt and rearranged her cupboard space. You observe that one neighbor stores nested suitcases permanently in the trunk of the car. You see what appears to be a record cabinet on one wall of the living room, then discover that it contains not records, but Sunday-best china and glassware.

This searching out becomes a hobby with you. Having put together a dozen or more such ideas, you approach (by letter) the editor of a home-making publication. The editor regrets — and perhaps sincerely so — that he sees no way to use an article of this length and scope. He is, however, interested in having you get a photograph of that porch-closet for rain-gear.

Next you turn to your list of trade publications and little magazines (see marginal notes). You

When You Write An Article for a Magazine

Try this system: Narrow down your thinking to a topic sentence. Make that thought apparent in your first paragraph, then go on to expand, explain, and interpret that basic thought. Every magazine article is, of course, an experiment, but in almost every instance this is a good course to consider.

send the cupboard idea to one that has to do with building materials. You send the suitcase idea to a trade magazine devoted to travel or touring. And so on, until you have put most of your material into motion. You do it all in a spirit of passing along ideas, knowing full well that the monetary rewards will probably be slight indeed. But you have enjoyed following through on your project.

There is another valid reason for making contact with editors, whether immediate sales are made or not. Very often an editor needs an "editorial errand" executed in your locality, and, having observed the quality of your work and the personality of your letters, he may give you the assignment.

The thing is, if you want to write you will write. And everything that you do write, whether it is published or isn't, gives you fresh insight into the world around you.

Suggestions for Students

Are you a student, hoping eventually to find a place on the editorial staff of a magazine? Then you, too, must specialize in ways such as the following:

During your years in school become well-grounded in your home economics specialty. Learn all you can about writing. Practice doing recipes, directions, and other forms of expository writing. Go over everything you write, editing and revamping your copy until it is crystal clear. Take up photography as a hobby and experiment with it. Learn to use a typewriter. Develop an awareness of what goes on around you. Think creatively.

One young home economist being interviewed for a job in the foods department of a national magazine remarked that she had wondered how

---

QUESTION BOX

Q. Do I need a literary agent to market my how-to-do-it articles?
A. No. A good agent is a definite help in marketing books, fiction, and articles of general appeal, but is not necessary for how-to-do-it material.

Q. What shall I do if an editor asks me to make changes in my copy?
A. Make them cheerfully. Remember, every editor knows her own magazine's policies and aims. You, an outsider, cannot possibly know t h e s e things.

Q. What shall I do if an editor changes my copy?
A. Nothing. That's her privilege.

Q. If I do not hear from an editor within a month, shall I write her?
A. No. Be patient a little longer. She may be on a trip, or your article may be routed to other editors for consideration. Most editors are quite prompt about returning unsuitable articles.

a certain photographic effect had been achieved in one of the magazine pages. This told the editor that here was a girl who had awareness. Eventually in the course of conversation, the applicant mentioned that at one time she had photographed pieces of colored cloth to see how each color would appear in a black-and-white photograph. By this time the editor sensed that the girl had a creative mind.

Yes, the young home economist got the job and has worked happily ever after.

Let us hope, then, that a number of you reading this will one day be considered "editorial timber" by a homemaking editor. Let us hope, too, that some of you who are now homemakers may realize your ambition of seeing your writing published.

If and when such hopes materialize, you must consider another fact. If you are to be on the staff of a publication, you must learn to work with others. If you are an outside contributor, you must accept the fact that what you write will probably be rewritten. Some of your most precious words may be weeded out. You may be disappointed in the way your copy is cut, but you must still cooperate.

Keep in mind, always, that every present-day magazine is an example of what might be termed "distilled journalism." In a foods department, for example, the foods editor knows several weeks ahead of publication date just how many columns of space she will have at her disposal. Months ahead, she knows what subjects she wants to feature. She sets one or more of the staff home economists to work, creating, testing, and retesting the recipes to be used. Others go "prop" hunting for the photographs. Everyone in the department adds ideas. Everyone taste-tests the recipes. Eventually the material is put together, only to be checked and edited again by the copy-editors. No

SLANTS AND CYCLES

Every magazine has its special slant. Try to figure out what it is for each publication that interests you. At the same time remember that editorial material seems to run in cycles. For a time, copy may be written in almost smarty fashion, then swing back to simplicity. For a time a magazine may use only staff-written material, then all of a sudden encourage outside contributions. Don't be too concerned about cycles — they'll change.

PREPARING THAT MANUSCRIPT

1. Use good grade typing paper of standard size — 8½" x 11".
2. Put your name and address in the upper left-hand corner of first page.
3. In opposite c o r n e r state approximate number of words.
4. Put title and sub-title in middle of first page, about 4 inches from top of page. Then proceed.
5. Double-space between the line.
6. Number the pages.
7. Keep a carbon. Keep a record of where manuscript was sent, and when; also a record of payment when it is sold.
8. Save that carbon until article has appeared in print.

one person on a magazine can be all-important. All must synchronize their ideas with those of others.

No book can tell you what to write, or prophesy whether or not what you write will be published. What this book wishes to emphasize is this:

Develop awareness of magazines — not only of the ones you see most frequently, but of smaller publications as well. Realize that while all home-appeal magazines are edited by a staff of specialists, most editors' doors and minds are open to really new, interesting, and practical ideas. Learn to think creatively — particularly in developing your own specialities. Be willing to merge your thinking with that of others. Learn to write clearly. Don't get discouraged. If you do these, your dream of working on or for a magazine may eventually become a reality.

MAILING A MANUSCRIPT

If manuscript is six pages or less, fold it in thirds and send it first class in a long business envelope.

Enclose stamps for possible return. Better yet, send a stamped, self-addressed envelope.

If manuscript runs six to ten pages, fold it once and use a 7" x 9" heavy manuscript envelope.

If manuscript is more than ten pages, or if there are photos, send it flat in a 9" x 12" envelope, with cardboard for protection.

THE HIGH COST OF COMMUNICATIONS

It is well for each of us to give thought to the economics of home economics; to ponder the staggering cost of furthering home economics education and home economics communications. It does us good to face up to what it costs to maintain our departments; to figure, even roughly, what it means in dollars and cents to bring out and distribute a leaflet or to put out an information release; to make a typographical change in a piece of copy after the presses are set to go.

Such figuring reminds us that when we produce photographs or sets of words that are not usable, or that are lost on the homemaker or student, we have wasted a great deal of someone's money. We have not lived up to the economics side of our profession. G.A.C.

15.

Advertising

How to develop
sales sense

PRACTICALLY EVERY HOME ECONOMIST employed by a business firm must work with her own company's advertising and sales promotion departments, and usually also with the advertising agency handling the firm's account. She has to think in terms of selling her company's product.

As a business home economist, your responsibility is to help copy writers and layout men do the most effective job of presenting your firm's product to homemakers. That means you must supply them with material which they can use to advantage: ideas, suggestions, recipes, etc., that will best sell the product. Also, you must help them — as unobtrusively and unofficiously as possible — to express and illustrate those ideas in ways that will have most meaning and greatest appeal to homemakers. Your position is an important one, for you must be as good a diplomat as you are a home economist.

The preparation of any advertisement or campaign in which a home economist participates is a three-cornered affair — a triangle made up of

*An advertisement
is a central idea
poured into an attractive
mold and garnished with interest.*

the copy department on one side, the art department on another, and the home economics department on the third side. No one department works by itself. The other two are involved in practically every move or decision and all must center around the client and his product.

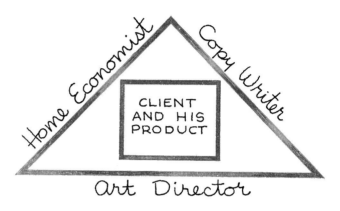

This situation, like other triangles in human relations, can cause problems if not thoroughly understood and wisely handled. Copy writers and layout men may get an idea that the home economist is trying to tell them what and how to do. The home economist may get an idea that she is a mere flunky to those other departments. A complete understanding of each other's responsibilities and of how these fit together is necessary in order to avoid ruffled feelings and time-and-energy-wasting friction. As an example, here roughly is the way the development of a food advertisement proceeds, at least in some agencies:

Granted that the basic approach of the campaign has been established, someone has an idea for an ad or a series of ads. It may be that one of the layout men has an inspiration for a certain type of illustration. He works up a rough layout, submits it to the higher-ups — the ones who deal directly with the client. If they consider it worth

EVERY HOME ECONOMIST IS IN ADVERTISING

Teachers, extension home economists, t e a r o o m managers, dietitians, finance counselors, business home economists — all sell their ideas and projects. Hence, every home economist is in the advertising b u s i n e s s, needs to understand the true meaning of the term.

exploring, the home economist is called in to suggest dishes that will carry out the idea, and to develop recipes from which one or more can be selected to feature in the advertisement. The copy department is put to work on headlines and selling copy.

Or it may be that one of the copy writers has a bright idea for a headline or a particular copy slant which the agency heads feel should be worked up. In that case the home economist may be called in for her ideas before the art department is brought in, or vice versa.

Or it may be that the home economist herself suggests a new line of uses for the product in the home kitchen, or a fresh presentation of the basic uses. She submits her idea, accompanied by a memo giving her reasoning. It is fortified by a list of possible recipes to be developed, any one of which could make a dramatic photograph, and would be appealing and practical for home use. If her suggestion is thought important enough for further consideration, the layout and copy departments are called in to discuss the matter and work up roughs.

The important thing, so far as agency executives are concerned, is the idea. They want it to be soundly practical from the homemaker's point of view, of course. But that is not enough. It must have something about it that stops the casual reader, causes her to look twice, to read, to make up her mind favorably in regard to the product featured. Those executives are concerned with sales. You must sense — and develop — that same concern.

When you, a home economist, first begin working with an advertising agency, you are not likely to be asked for your ideas on an advertisement or campaign. Instead, you probably will be told exactly what the layout and copy chiefs want from you. That holds true, ordinarily, whether

SURVEYS SHOW . . .

In magazine advertising, photographs seem to attract more attention than do other forms of art. . . . Food advertisments which feature recipes set so that they *look* like recipes attract higher readership than do food advertisements without recipes. Yes, the home economist is important in the advertising business.

you are employed full-time, or part-time as a free lance home economist or consultant.

Should you offer an idea when you have not been asked? That question cannot be answered with a blanket statement. Generally speaking, you will get along better and faster if you are not too quick in volunteering suggestions, too didactic and officious in saying just what you think ought to be done and how. Remember, copy writers and art directors are much more familiar with the techniques and the results of advertising than you — an amateur or outsider in the business — can possibly be.

DIRECTORIES

"American Business Directory" and "Trade and Professional Associations of the United States" are valuable references for analyzing the business market. Both are sold by the United States Government Printing Office, Washington 25, D.C.

It is better, usually, to proceed slowly. Prove to your employers that you can produce good recipes and photographic setups to carry out ideas originated by the creative department. If someone suggests something that you feel would be over-elaborate, or out-of-date, or otherwise impractical or unsuitable for use, don't flatly condemn it. Instead, show that you have good judgment — and good manners, too — by quietly offering another and better possibility. Prove that you can produce material that makes good selling copy and illustrations, and eventually you will find that you are being asked for ideas before a campaign is planned — at least before the copy slants and layouts are completely jelled.

You can't force yourself, can't force the recognition you desire. But you can speed it up by working to improve yourself. Here are some pointers you can follow to make yourself more valuable, less vulnerable.

1. Keep learning more and more about home-making women and what their interests are. Keep in touch with individual homemakers — your own relatives, friends, acquaintances — and with other home economists in editorial work, extension, utility and appliance companies, and the like, who are in touch with large numbers of women.

2. Keep learning more and more about how artists and layout persons and copy creators work and think. Visit with them. Ask intelligent questions; listen intently. The better you understand their problems, the better you will be able to co-operate with them, and the less likely you are to be irked by things they do or do not do.

3. Do advance thinking about accounts on which you are working, and problems you know are coming up. Keep a growing file of ideas that you know are good from the homemaker's standpoint, and that have the makings of good selling copy and illustration.

4. Before presenting an idea, figure out what approach is best for the particular executive with whom you are working.

With some types of persons, the best way is to drop a thought casually in conversation, and see if it strikes a spark. You may not get any reaction at the moment, or ever. On the other hand, you may hear your idea brought up days or weeks later, with or without credit to you. But don't worry about credit. Just be proud if your idea is considered good enough to use.

With other types of executives, it's best to wait until you are asked for ideas. When you are, then sort out the best of those on your list and examine them closely to see that they would really sell the product. Ask yourself these questions about each one:

WHAT'S IN A NAME?

A great deal. Give appealing names to recipes that are to appear in advertising. Make them headlines in themselves.

(a) Will this recipe or idea do a really good job for the product? If you are working on a flour advertisement, for example, does your recipe call for a reasonably large amount of flour such as for cake, pie, or rolls? Does it show off the quality of the flour to best advantage?

(b) Does the goodness of the recipe depend chiefly on the product, or is the product merely something added that can be omitted all too easily?

(c) Is the recipe or idea in step with the times? Will everything called for in the recipe be generally available and reasonably priced at the time the advertisement appears?

(d) Will the finished dish photograph well?

(e) Is it the kind of dish that has not only those qualities that make for quick interest and appeal, but also that make for long-lasting favoritism?

5. Never forget that the best selling copy for any home product shows how the product is useful in solving problems for homemakers. Never forget that you are the one who must interpret those homemakers to your advertising chiefs. Never forget that such interpreting carries with it great responsibility.

The Other Side of the Picture

Some of you who read this chapter may not be home economists, but copy writers producing copy directed to homemakers. You are wondering how you can best work with a home economist to make most effective use of her training and experience.

That home economist, whether she is on the staff of your client or is working for your agency full-time or on a free-lance or consultant basis, has three things to offer you: (1) judgment; (2) skills; (3) ideas. The better use you make of all three, the more your copy is likely to appeal to and influence homemakers.

The question, of course, is how to do this. Here are recommendations offered by advertising executives and experienced home economists.

1. Make sure that you (the producer of the copy or campaign) and the home economist are visualizing the same sort of homemakers. To the home economist, the typical homemaker is a wife and mother who takes her home job rather seri-

WHEN IT'S DANGEROUS TO BE FANCY

When an experienced homemaker sees a picture of an ultra-fancy cake or concoction, she knows at a glance whether it is practical from her standpoint. The inexperienced homemaker lacks this background of information; lacks skills. She is more likely to try out strange ideas and is often disappointed that they do not come out as pictured. It is bad business to disappoint young homemakers, for they are forming buying habits that will stay with them for years to come.

ously. The copy writer — particularly if she is young and inexperienced — may think of homemakers as being always on the alert for something fancy and strange, rather than useful and practical. The executive is likely to have a very definite and special type of homemaker in mind, frequently represented by *"my wife."* The important thing is that the art department, copy creators, and home economist all think in terms of the same type of homemaker and of what she will be thinking and doing at the time the advertisement appears. This means building a composite picture of the homemakers to whom the advertisement is addressed.

2. Make sure that the home economist has a complete picture of the entire job, not just her part in it. Make sure she understands — and believes in — the basis of the campaign. It is not good if a home economist is asked to provide "six recipes calling for the product," with no information as to where and how those recipes are to be used. When that is the case, the home economist provides only her skills — not her full judgment or ideas.

In some cases the home economist is asked to provide ideas to fit into a copy slant or campaign which she cannot whole-heartedly accept. When that is true, perhaps the slant needs to be re-examined; perhaps it merely needs to be made more clear to the home economist. But so long as she is unconvinced as to the complete soundness of the approach, her contributions are bound to be unconvincing.

3. Go over the proposed layouts with the home economist before the layouts and copy are completely settled. Let her see exactly how much space is allowed for presenting the photographs and ideas.

Keep in mind that it is a serious mistake to try to reduce the wordage of certain recipes. Either

KNOW, DON'T GUESS

Every home economist who works with or in advertising must remember that advertising copy, even though it may seem spontaneous, has been thought through carefully, is based on facts and figures. Be prepared to back up any statements you may make when rendering an opinion on advertising approaches.

the dish itself must be changed, a different approach to the recipe must be taken, or the layout must be altered. Many an excellent recipe or idea has been made unintelligible — if not completely inaccurate — by trying to reduce it to too few words. Unless a recipe makes sense to the reader, it is better to use no recipe at all.

4. Think twice before you insist that the home economist carry out too literally your own personal ideas on food preparation or recipe originations. What you want from her is judgment — not blind or bland submission. Many food ideas that taste fine on paper and look fine in photographs turn out to be quite impractical from the home kitchen standpoint.

Think twice, too, before you completely rewrite the home economist's copy. If you do, you may easily alter the sense of it. Question her, of course, on anything that does not come through clearly when you read it. One of the big jobs in preparing home economics copy is to make it real and convincing. Too much fussing around on the part of the home economist, too much working over of the copy by anyone or everyone, is likely to make the words sound glib, unreal, unconvincing.

5. Remember that working triangle discussed earlier in this chapter. Work to keep it a fairly equilateral triangle, with layout department, copy writer, and home economist sharing almost equal responsibility for the finished ad.

There's a saying that no work of art is ever done by a committee. But that is not strictly true. There are many cases where a skilled copy writer, an inspired layout department, and an ideaful yet practical home economist have worked together to create advertising of triple strength and close-harmony artistry.

16.

Cookbooks and Texts

How to weigh
the many problems

CONSIDERING the long lists of cookbooks currently on the market and the new ones constantly pouring in from publishers' presses, it might seem that to write another cookbook would be to take a great big gamble. And it is!

But, you say, some persons who write cookbooks do win against all the odds, do make money and gain prestige. That, too, is true.

Before you jump to conclusions, however, analyze the situation. Perhaps that new, best-selling book is backed (directly or indirectly) by some company willing to invest heavily in promoting it. Perhaps the author has hit upon a really new subject that would have wide appeal. Perhaps hers will be a "personality" approach — if she is a national figure in fiction or in some other field. Perhaps she is equipped to publicize her book through a chain of restaurants or cooking schools or lectures. There is usually some reason (other than its containing reliable, well-written recipes) that makes a new cookbook an outstanding success.

All factors should be carefully weighed before you consider writing any book!

Private Printing

Should you have a cook-book privately printed? There is no complete answer to that question. If you do contemplate such a step, better make it a small book that can be sold at a sensible price. Know in advance exactly what the book is going to cost to produce and how you are going to sell and distribute it. A book done by a group can be a collection of miscellaneous recipes; one done by an individual should, ordinarily, be swung around some one subject, as "Canapes and Appetizers."

You have, shall we say, realized all this, and still you are convinced that your cookbook idea will be a winner. You are certain that you have enough unique material to make an interesting book. What do you do first?

First step is to make a study of books on the market. Look over the assortment of cookbooks in all of the book stores and book departments in your community. Study titles, tables of contents, and layout. Talk with men and women who sell books. Talk with librarians. Study catalogs or lists from various cookbook publishers.

As you see and study that vast accumulation of books, and lists of books, ask yourself the next question: "Does my idea duplicate too many other cookbooks on the market?"

If it doesn't, and if you still feel your idea is a new and right one, ask yourself that biggest question of all: "Can I afford to gamble 6 to 12 months of writing time, plus costs of recipe testing, art work, typing, etc., against the possible royalties I may receive from sales?" Figure it out. How many books would you have to sell, at somewhere around 30 to 50 cents royalty on each book, to repay that investment and pay a profit? Can you sensibly hope to sell that many books?

These questions and comments are not intended to discourage you. They are meant to help you recognize facts and possibilities, and make up your mind on the basis of knowledge rather than mere hope.

Having faced all of these, you may wish to pursue the project further. Now what?

At this stage in the proceedings, you'd better begin querying book publishers. You have been studying cookbooks everywhere, jotting down addresses of publishing companies, writing them for descriptive brochures on the cookbooks they put out. You check through those titles to see that your idea has not already been covered thoroughly. Or, if your idea is an adaptation of a more or less standard subject, such as quantity cookery, you will cross off every publisher who already has a relatively new book on the subject. If he already has a quantity cookbook, he is not likely to want to bring out another one to compete with the first.

Pick a publisher whose books appeal to you as being well done: well edited, and typographically and artistically inviting. Write that publisher — and at this time only that one publisher — the best letter you can work out. Tell him enough about your idea so that he can judge whether his company would care to go into the matter further. Give him your table of contents, tell him whom your book is aimed for — specifically — and what's distinctive about it. Tell him about yourself, too — your experience, your previously published books or articles, etc. — so he can judge whether you are enough of a writer, enough of an authority to write on your chosen subject.

You may be sure your letter is telling him a great deal more about yourself than you know. It tells him whether your mind is clear and sharp, or foggy or lazy. It tells him whether you are thinking of the book from the publisher's standpoint of *selling* and the reader's standpoint of *buying,* or merely from your own personal wish to see a book with your name on bookstore shelves.

If that particular publisher says he is not interested, try another, and so on — one at a time in order of your preference. If no publisher wants it, you may feel pretty sure it is considered a poor risk from the sales standpoint. You'd better forget the whole thing and turn to something else without feeling too much disappointment. But file your material away carefully. You are almost certain to find a use for it later!

If a publisher does express interest, he will tell you what he wants next from you. It probably will

Group Effort

Is your church or club group planning to put out a cookbook? If so, you must have an editor in charge, plus an editorial staff. There must be a production person to follow through; a financial committee to check costs and see to it that the book is kept within that budget; a sales committee to sell the book; and a publicity person to get the book before the general public.

TIMING

Planning to do a cookbook? Better allow 6 to 12 months for writing it; another 2 or 3 months for ironing out details with the publisher, and perhaps up to a year for manufacturing the book and launching it.

be a complete outline with as big a sample of the manuscript as you can provide. Unless you're already an established "name," the samples are going to be the basis for decision, rather than merely the idea.

To work up your outline and sample chapters, you must now start on that big task of seriously organizing your material.

If you think of a cookbook as a *collection of booklets,* you will find it easier to begin the job of planning the book and organizing your material. Think of each chapter as a booklet devoted to just one phase or segment of the general subject.

Set up an assortment of folders, one for each of the proposed chapters. Distribute your collected recipes among them. As you work, you will weed out some that seem too commonplace, others that do not quite seem to belong in the pattern that is forming more clearly in your mind. You will think of other recipes that the book seems to need. You will have ideas for dishes that you could work out to make those chapters more unique, interesting, and valuable to the readers. All this comes to mind while you are thoughtfully sorting and distributing recipes, rather than merely refiling them in an unthinking, routine way.

From here on it is a matter of how well you can organize that outline, how well you can write. Once you get this material to the publisher, the decision rests with him. A word of advice is in order here: take plenty of time to work out that outline and sample. They must be right before you let them go.

If and when the idea is really accepted, a contract will be forwarded to you to study and sign. Then there will be more conferences and more correspondence to iron out various problems and to shape and dramatize the book the way that

TITLE CHECK

Think twice before you decide on a cookbook title that does not contain one of these three words: *cook, cooking,* or *recipes.* If you wish to check on whether your proposed title has been used previously look in the *Cumulative Book Index* and *Books in Print,* drawn from the *Publishers' Trade List Annual,* in your library or large book store or book department. Also check *Publishers' Weekly* for titles of books just off the press or about to be published.

THE PUBLISHER

There's a difference between publishing and printing. A publisher is one who has the organization to help with editing the manuscript and handle details of planning and production, as well as the machinery not only to manufacture books, but to promote, distribute, and sell them to dealers. He usually takes his own risk financially, pays a royalty on books sold. A printer almost never assumes such responsibility. He merely follows orders.

seems best to both. Compromises will be necessary. New ideas will be injected, to be rejected or adopted or adapted.

Eventually you will have a definite mental picture of the book to work toward. You will know the number of pages, and other necessary details. You will know the date when the manuscript must be in the publisher's hands and the scheduled publication date. You will have worked out a fairly definite outline for the arrangement of chapters and of material within each chapter. Now you are ready to produce.

Get off to a good start. Begin with something especially appetizing and appealing, rather than with page after page of glossaries, definitions of cookery terms, tables of vitamins and minerals, prosy and obvious advice about how to plan meals or equip kitchens. No one knows how many possible sales are discouraged by dull beginnings, but door-to-door book salesmen say that the appearance of the opening pages of a book determines whether they make a quick sale or no sale at all. Salesmen in book departments say the same thing!

In writing, get freshness and originality in your wording. But be wary of labored cuteness as you are wary of using slang or hackneyed phrases. Don't work too consciously to develop a style of writing. Instead, work for simple clearness and unaffected freshness. The less obtrusive, less "put on" a style is, the better it is. Write to a person, and you are not likely to go wrong, so far as style is concerned. Above all, don't write in a hurried way, even though you are working against a deadline.

Send your manuscript to the publisher in the best possible shape but be prepared to work on it further, as his editors come up with good ideas. Keep a carbon copy so you can exchange thoughts and answer questions. Your book is on its way!

WHAT ABOUT COPYRIGHTS?

Cookbooks are frequently copyrighted in the author's name. Most other books are copyrighted by the publisher. A copyright in the United States endures for 28 years, may then be renewed for another 28 years. The publisher takes care of having the book copyrighted. If you want to have a privately printed book copyrighted, get Application Form A from the Register of Copyrights, Library of Congress, Washington 25, D.C. Free.

"Copyright Law of the U.S.A." may be purchased for 15 cents from the Superintendent of Documents, U. S. Government Printing Office, Washington 25, D.C.

ROYALTIES

Most contracts call for starting payments to the author of any book at 10 per cent of the retail price, with arrangements for a slightly higher rate after a certain sales volume has been reached.

Other Types of Home Economics Books

TO PREPARE AN INDEX

1. Go through page proofs of books carefully, underlining in blue pencil all words to be indexed. Underline sub-entries in red pencil. Make marginal notes of items to be cross-indexed. This done, you are ready to figure the general plan of the index.
2. Go through proofs again, this time making a card for each underlined word and each item to be cross-indexed. (Cards 3x5 inches are a good size to handle.) Be accurate in making up these cards; note page numbers carefully.
3. Arrange cards alphabetically, using a box that allows room for re-arranging.
4. Using a well-indexed book as a guide, go through the cards; consolidate the entries, then type them, following the style decided upon.
5. Check carbon copy of index against marked-up page-proofs.

CHEERFUL NOTE

Not all buyers of cookbooks are users of them. Some are collectors who buy every interesting new cookbook or every one along a certain line. Happily, this group helps to swell sales — and royalties!

These rules of effective writing apply also to writing in other home economics fields: sewing, child development, home decorating, arts and crafts, gardening, and other types of home how-to-do-its. That is, the textbook, like the cookbook, may be considered a collection of booklets or lessons, each a unit in itself, yet a part of the over-all subject. The textbook, however, more frequently is written to order, because a publisher has seen a need. But an author may have sensed this need and written on her own initiative to fill what to her is a void.

This chapter in this book dealing with writing for homemakers is not the place to go into complete detail on writing the home economics text. But if you are working on a textbook, give earnest thought to the following questions. Prospective publishers will be considering these points as they examine your manuscript in light of a need and the filling of a need:

1. *For whom is the book intended?* Write for one person — preferably a real person whom you know — rather than for "a broad, general audience." Write for a definite *one* and your publisher may reach thousands. But write for thousands and you may be so indefinite as not to *reach* one.

2. *Does it fit the needs of great numbers of teachers in reaching students?* Keep point No. 1 in mind here — from the teacher's standpoint. The student is the one to be reached, of course, but it must be done through the teacher.

3. *Does this book really teach?* A number of textbooks now in use are made up of discussions about subject matter rather than of lessons to be learned and applied.

4. *Does it recognize current teaching methods?*
Great changes are being wrought in education. The textbook writer must be in step with the times — certainly not behind. Right now the trend is toward choosing simple material and presenting it simply. "Education for today's living" is the usual keynote of freshest, newest books on homemaking — foods, textiles, and the like.

Educators are recognizing that the student does not need to learn everything that the teacher knows. Thus texts and reference books now tend to emphasize the pertinent facts and procedures a student needs to know, and to show her how to put her new knowledge into everyday practice.

There is perhaps less telling the student to act in a certain way, more setting up of typical homemaking problems and coaching the student how to search out or reason out the best answers. At least that is one aim.

5. *Is the style of writing fresh and up-to-date?* Is it informal yet dignified? Is it clear cut? Is there variety in sentence length, with a minimum of long, involved sentences? Are the words simple and meaningful, rather than empty syllables?

6. *Will this book be of permanent value to the reader?* Will she want to keep it and refer to it because it offers something she will not find elsewhere — at least in so usable a fashion?

Once you feel reasonably certain that the text you visualize does live up to these requirements, you are ready to approach a textbook publisher by letter. He will probably proceed much as the publisher of cookbooks proceeds. From then on it is a matter of working out details with him, provided he is interested in what you have to offer.

One other thing might be added here. If you

WHAT ABOUT FICTIONIZED COOKBOOKS?

Some successful cookbooks for children and some for adults have been written in story form. Generally speaking, however, the direct, non-fictionized approach is preferred by publishers and by cookbook buyers.

HOW TO REVIEW A COOKBOOK

Along with giving a word picture of the book and what is in it, tell why it will appeal to certain types of readers. Never base your opinion of it on your own personal likes and dislikes. If you don't care for it, why mention it at all? Adverse comment, particularly when written in smarty vein, does no one any good.

LOOKING AHEAD TO REVISION

Many cookbooks and most textbooks need to be revised from time to time. It's a good idea for the author to keep a revision copy at hand, writing in marginal notes or changes or additions to be made when a revised edition is brought out.

are seriously interested in doing some special text, make it a point to attend national and state home economics conventions and to study the textbooks on display at such conventions. Brief chats with the publishers' representatives in charge of such book displays frequently lead to serious discussions and, later, to contracts!

COMPARATIVE SIZES OF TYPE

This is a sample of 6 point type (solid). As you can see, type of this size is hard to read — especially in a line the length of this. It is sometimes used for captions — especially on a small page. But 8 point solid is preferable.

This is 8 point solid, set for comparison with the paragraph above to show the difference effected.

This is 8 point on a 9 point body. (In other words, there is a little "air" between the lines.) Although it is small, it works well in small blocks of copy.

This is 9 point type on a 10 point body This, or 9 solid, is frequently used for recipes or leaflets.

This is 10 point solid in Baskerville face. It is easy to read and usually a better choice than 8 point or 9 point. In this particular type face, 10 point is satisfactory when set *solid*, as in this sample. Other type faces may need a point or two of space between lines for best results. Set solid, 10 point runs 7 lines per inch; 8 point solid gives 9 lines per inch; 6 point solid gives 12 lines per inch. Type faces in general are better with 1- or 2-point spacing, however.

This is 10 point Primer set solid, for comparison with the 10 point Baskerville solid above. Notice that the feeling here is not as "comfortable" as in the Baskerville lines because the face is bigger.

The pages of this book are set in 10 point Primer on 12-point body, giving 6 lines per inch. The face is one which is improved by some spacing, as shown here.

"Some cook b o o k s are primarily reading cookbooks, others are cooking cookbooks. Some, happily, are both."

"There are three things a cookbook needs if it is to sell: (1) fresh point of view; (2) personality; (3) steady promotion."

"We have a standard by which we judge cookbooks. Do the recipes make us hungry and impatient to start experimenting? If they don't, we tend to suspect the book."

TRENDS IN TEXTBOOKS

Current practice is to put home economics facts and procedures into simple home language instead of the stilted, impersonal scientese so long considered the correct way to write a textbook.

The trend, too, is toward writing textbooks that tie in with visual aid programs (films, slides, and the like); or vice versa, toward developing visual aids that tie in with textbooks.

17.

Speeches and Programs

How to tailor a talk
to fit a group

WHATEVER YOUR HOME ECONOMICS JOB, there are sure to be times in your career when you must give a speech. It may be to a small group of salesmen or to an audience of homemakers or home economists. It may be limited to five minutes or extended to 45. Whatever the subject, the occasion, and the time allowed, you want that speech to be a good one.

The task becomes easier, and the speech more effective, when you look at it from three angles:

1. Planning and writing the speech.
2. Figuring how to bring the speech to life.
3. Giving the speech.

How To Plan a Speech

Your first step in planning is not to think about what you will say. It is to think about who is going to hear you. Visualize that audience first; then ask yourself, "What can I say that will be of special interest to this particular group on this particular occasion?"

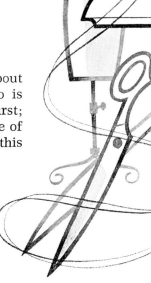

Tailor your talk or program
to fit the group.
And don't be afraid
to use the scissors!

If you are to speak to homemakers, for example, get a mental picture of those homemakers and their problems. If you are to address a gathering of dietitians or of teachers, think in terms of what such professionals would want to hear. What you have to say may be basically the same for each group, but your approach will be quite different. When you visualize an audience clearly, you not only make sure that your speech will be more flattering to your listeners, but also will be easier for you to plan. And when you actually give your speech, you will find that thinking of those listeners rather than of yourself has helped you to get rid of your own self-consciousness.

AVOID THE ABSTRACT APPROACH

When you give a speech the temptation often is to talk in the abstract. Resist that temptation. Instead, talk to persons; use personal experiences. The more lifeless the subject matter, the more necessary it is to put life into its presentation.

PICK AN APPEALING TITLE

Having visualized your audience and decided in a general way about your subject matter, stop right then and there and figure out what to call your talk. Why do it at that time? For two reasons. First, once the title is in your mind, it acts as a magnet, picking up significant facts and interesting incidents that can be woven into the speech. Second, the sooner you have a good title, the sooner publicity about your talk can get under way. The more your subject or title is mentioned in publicity, the greater the anticipation the audience builds up for what you have to say. And, of course, the *better* the title, the better the publicity and the anticipation.

That title must sound alive, not static. It must be specific, not general. It must be provocative, or at least arouse curiosity. It must make everyone who reads it say, "Now that is something I really want to hear."

For example, you are to speak to young business women on the subject of nutrition. If you choose the title, "Meals for Maximum Nutrition," you will stir up absolutely no excitement in the minds of those girls. That's a take-it-or-leave-it title, and too many will decide to leave it. But if you put your emphasis on the girls and their interests and call your talk something like, "Eat Right and Stay Slim," or "Eat Right and Be Beautiful," you'll have the audience with you even before you begin speaking.

Thinking up a just-right title is hard work, but it's worth doing. Remember, a good strong handle makes it possible for you to pick up your thoughts and put them down right where they belong.

MAKE AN OUTLINE YOUR AUDIENCE CAN FOLLOW

In planning any speech you will, of course, decide on the three or four or five main points you wish to get across. Those points are the outline — which is something a speech absolutely must have if it is to hang together and be effective. Now, how can you help your audience to keep that outline in mind?

Simplest way to do this is to state, at the beginning, the points you are going to cover; then go ahead and elaborate on each in that order. It's the pattern of "tell 'em what you're going to tell 'em; then tell 'em."

Incidentally, here is a little trick or device: Plan to develop your first main point rather quickly, then take more time, as needed, on the others. Why? Because at the beginning of a lecture an audience is eager and curious and a bit restless; it wants action. When you cover your first point quickly, your audience feels pleased because your talk is evidently going to march along.

When you get into the second point you can slow down, expand ideas more fully, work in plenty of illustrations and incidents. By this time your audience is used to your voice, is into the

---

TITLES FOR TALKS

The good speech title usually suggests how a problem might be solved (such as "How To Manage a Budget"); or it gets in the *you* approach (such as "How To Be Your Own Decorator"); or it indicates news (such as "Trends in Home Decorating" or "New Color Schemes for Kitchens"). Other good words to use in titles are: Today; Tomorrow; Why; Where.

WARNING

Beware of such pretentious titles as these: "Helping Adolescents Obtain Social Skills," and "Techniques in Evaluating Home Economics Presentations." These are scientese words and phrases.

spirit of your speech. Also you will have felt out the audience, sensed its reactions. As you go into the remaining points you can build them up or cut them down, depending on the time available and the responsiveness of your listeners.

Make sure that the main points of your speech are parallel in construction. In that speech to the business girls, called "Eat and Stay Slim," for example, the points in your outline might be something like this:

> How much food does a business girl need?
> What foods are necessary in a well-rounded diet?
> Which of these foods build bone and muscle tissues rather than fat?
> What type of daily diet will keep weight down, energy up?

Note those key words: *How, What, Which, What.* See how they hold the outline together; how they keep it parallel in construction. Remember, the sharper your outline, the easier it is for you to develop and the easier it is for the audience to follow.

ADDED INDUCEMENT

A man or woman prominent in public life often can be induced to speak before a group, provided the speech later is to be published in a professional journal.

BRING POINTS TO LIFE

Once you have the outline of what you are going to say, it's time to think about dramatizing — bringing to life — the points in that outline. Here are several ways to do so:

Point up your ideas with examples. In this way you avoid preaching. You *show* rather than tell.

Use illustrative materials whenever feasible. Exhibits such as drapery samples in a talk on home decorating, and charts to clarify facts or figures in a presentation on household finance, have helped to liven up many a talk that would otherwise have been slow.

Work in plenty of personal incidents — not cut-and-dried stories, unless you can tell them unusually well, but pertinent little anecdotes that the audience will remember.

Follow the fiction writer's tricks of foreshadowings and flashbacks to weave your points together. For example, "I'll have more to say about this when we come to our third point." Or, "You will recall that earlier I mentioned such and such."

Compliment the audience. Instead of saying, "I saw a cartoon the other day," say, "You probably saw the cartoon . . ." This is just the gracious, thoughtful way of putting others ahead of yourself in your thinking. Avoid overusing that pronoun "I." When you must use it, be careful not to over-emphasize it, as "*I* think," "*I* believe," and so on.

Questions To Ask Yourself

One way to make your audiences sit up and take notice (as well as take notes) is to test every speech in advance by asking yourself four questions. This is a test used, consciously or unconsciously, by every successful speaker.

IS THERE ANYTHING IN MY SPEECH WORTH QUOTING?

A reporter on a metropolitan newspaper was asked what, in her opinion, constituted a speech worthy of advance or follow-up publicity in her paper. "I always look for at least one quotable statement that could make a headline," she answered. "If it isn't there, I skip the story."

If you want to test the truth of that statement, study the reports of meetings as they appear in your local papers. See if most of the stories about speeches don't bring out some pertinent facts brought out by the speaker.

Then study your own speech. Are you saying anything of sufficient importance to be repeated — either in print, or orally by those who listen to you? Could you, if you were a reporter, write a story built around your pearly words of wis-

CHARTS AND POSTERS

Reduce your wordage to a minimum. Consider color and its effect. Black on yellow, for example, has a high degree of visibility. In hand-lettering, print the first letter of a word, then the last letter; then the letters in between. If you do, spacing will work out better.

USING A CHALK BOARD?

Be sure the chalk board is washed clean and that there's an eraser and plenty of chalk. Experiment in advance to see how large your writing or lettering should be. Avoid long, involved sentences; keep your blackboard copy to outline form.

LITTLE THINGS THAT COUNT

Have a table or rostrum on the platform. No, you won't lean on it, but it gives you psychological support. Pick out some one person in the audience and speak directly to her or him. Shift your weight occasionally. Pause frequently to smile.

dom? If not, something more needs to be done to that speech. Put in several quotable lines, packed with meaning, and see if you haven't stepped up your talk at least fifty per cent.

HAVE I USED PLENTY OF EXAMPLES TO GET MY POINTS ACROSS?

Those of you who have listened to anyone talk at length on some general or abstract subject know what a relief it is when the speaker breaks the pattern with a story or incident or other illustration that lights up some important fact.

Think back to some of the talks you remember most vividly. What was there about them that impressed you? In many instances, didn't the speaker depend largely on some such device to bring his words to life, which in turn made you remember them?

Let's say you're to take part in a panel discussion on some phase of family relations. If you merely talk about family relations problems in general, your contribution to the panel is all too likely to parrot what others are saying. If, however, you talk about a few specific families and how they solved their specific but typical problems, your part of the panel discussion will have strength and importance.

One business home economist who is frequently invited to take part in convention meetings rarely builds a talk on her own personal experiences or convictions. Instead, she visits with homemakers, grocers, business executives — anyone and everyone — asking questions, seeking new slants on problems and their solutions. By doing this, she is not only able to give a different twist to her subject matter, but she puts breadth and depth into what she has to say. What's more, her platform manner is pleasing, because in quoting others, she loses all self-consciousness.

SPEECH-MAKING

Learn to make speeches. Accept invitations to give talks, so you will develop ability and poise. Making occasional speeches — good ones, that is — helps to build you professionally by making you more widely known, h e n c e more likely to be thought of when a good position is open.

Smile at the audience... Don't start out with an apology . . . Tell what you are going to say. . . Say it. . . Tell what you have said. . . Sit down. . . Don't thank the audience.

Study the points you hope to get across in that speech of yours. Are they going to come through clearly? Probably not, unless you clinch them with incidents, case histories, or other illustrations that catch and hold the interest of the audience.

IS MY SPEECH DOWN-TO-EARTH?

One weakness common to many of us is liking to show off a bit. When we give a speech there is sometimes the temptation to impress people with our knowledge of this or that.

We are not likely to yield to that temptation, however, when we keep the audience foremost in our thinking.

To be sure, it's a good idea to let a presentation of any kind fly high at a few points, but it's usually safest not to let it fly too long and too high before bringing it down to earth. At least that is the point of view taken by some of the most successful speakers.

IS MY TALK TOO HEAVY-HANDED?

Regardless of how much we want to get across our "message," we dare not overdo it. For the more we bear down on a subject, the less likely the audience is to bear up under it.

Once when leaving a talk about a certain food product, one homemaker said, "I really like (name of product) very much. I came today thinking I would get some new ideas for using it. But the way I feel right now, I don't care if I never see it again. . . ."

Here is an example of an earnest home economist who wanted to tell all she knew — and it was just too much.

Injecting a light touch into what you have to say isn't easy — but it must be done. Just as

ON THE OTHER SIDE

When you are in the audience rather than on the platform, be a good listener. Listen with your eyes as well as with your ears. Help the speaker do a better than ever job by showing your interest and approval in your face.

hard writing makes for easy reading, so does intelligent kneading of heavy facts bring out a yeasty lightness that is relished by everyone. There are no dull subjects, you know — only dull presentations of them.

"But how can one inject that lightness?" you ask. According to one professional, there are three good ways: (1) Don't tell everything there is to say about a subject. Instead, select some one segment and explore it with enthusiasm. (2) Figure out fresh ways of stating heavy facts. (3) Surprise the audience with an amusing or hilarious incident when it is least expected.

When You Give That Speech

Don't memorize your talk, word for word, unless you can make it sound as if you were talking naturally to a neighbor! Use notes if you need them; it's better than to flounder and grope for the next thought. If you must read your talk, make sure you read with life and expression, as if you were speaking freely and naturally. Important thing is to follow whichever system of delivery is right for *you*.

Make your talk march along. Use short sentences but not choppy ones. Change your pace from time to time. Pause occasionally to let a thought sink into the minds of the audience. Use live, pictorial words that mean something to the listeners. Avoid glittering generalities. Be careful not to overuse some pet phrase; for example, don't end every sentence with "and so forth."

Keep your voice natural. There is no surer way to kill your message than to use old-fashioned high-flown oratory.

Avoid rapid speaking. (Don't talk faster than 150 words a minute.) Forget about gestures. They'll come naturally when needed.

Look *at*, not through or over the heads of your audience. Make a point of looking at various individuals and try to catch their eyes. Communications on this personal level can win their response; their approval will spread quickly.

Yes, there are any number of rules and yardsticks that apply to speech-making. Enough of them to fill several books — which they do. But, after all, doesn't it all sift down to this:

If you really work to think out something that your particular audience would like to hear. . . . If you fill your talk with personality, without talking too much about yourself. . . . If you speak with enthusiasm in a voice that all can understand. . . . If you are sincere, and, at the same time, sensitive to the reactions of your audience. . . . If you know when to stop. . . . Then chances are strong that everyone will leave the room saying, "I wouldn't have missed that for anything."

When that happens, you can really take a bow. For you have made a good speech!

How To Plan a Program

Unlike the planning of a speech, which is pretty much a one-person affair, the planning of a program is almost certain to be a joint undertaking. Ordinarily a committee of at least three, often many more, persons must work together. The problem is not only to produce good ideas for the program, but to blend the best ideas of all concerned into an interesting, unified presentation.

Actual planning of the program, of course, begins as always with the audience and the occasion.

It's good sense to devote most of the first com-

PROGRAM STUNTS

One way to dramatize a long, rather heavy program is to stage stunts that do not steal time away from the show itself. For example, make it a "Red Hat Luncheon" or a "Wear - Your - Favorite - Flower" affair. Or tell everyone to bring along her favorite gadget to serve as a conversation piece during the meal.

To relieve monotony in the year's program for a group, make one meeting a workshop. For example: Your topic is modern housing. Suggest that the speaker work out his talk so that the audience actually draws plans and works out room arrangements.

mittee meeting to (1) a quick analysis of the types of persons who will make up the group; (2) a discussion of the general aim or objective of the meeting in question; (3) a listing of all the various subjects along that line which would be interesting and helpful to the group. After such discussion and pooling of miscellaneous ideas, the committee then can proceed much more rapidly and effectively to put together a really good program. The first big step is to decide on the *theme*.

BUILD YOUR PROGRAM AROUND A THEME

PROGRAM THEME THOUGHTS

Mrs. America Today. Possible subjects to be fitted into such a theme might include: "How and Where She Lives"; "How She Spends Her Money"; "How She Cooks and Keeps House"; "How She Dresses Her Family"; "What She Hopes."

Kitchen Planning Forum. Possible subjects might include: "How the Engineer Looks at the Job"; "How the Artist Sees It"; "What the Home Economist Expects"; "What the Homemaker Wants."

All-Family Style Show. Subjects might include: "Breakfast in the Patio"; "All Ready for Church"; "Now for an Afternoon in the Garden"; "And a Quiet Evening at Home." These are, of course, given merely as examples of how such subjects might be approached.

Planning a program around a central theme makes it easier for the committee to select speakers and to assign topics to them. It makes it easier for the speakers to slant their talks in the same general direction. It provides a peg on which to swing the publicity. It makes the printed or mimeographed program more forceful. It suggests a key for table decorations. It keeps the committees and the speakers from going off on tangents. And it holds the audience together.

"But what kind of theme?" you may ask. There are as many answers to that question as there are programs to be given.

Let's imagine that you are planning a joint home economics meeting of teachers, extension workers, and business home economists. You know that while all phases of home economics are of real concern to the entire audience, many special interests are represented. You reason, therefore, that it might be well to present discussions on each of three important special-interest subjects such as textiles, foods, and home equipment. You realize that it is impossible to discuss any of these subjects completely in the 15 to 20 minutes that can be allowed each speaker.

You therefore figure out a theme. It might be

that old favorite, "What's New" in each of the three fields represented. "What's the News" in the textile field — all about the new fabrics and how to use them; in food products — examples and samples of new items; in home equipment — descriptions of the new ranges and refrigerators, or new ideas in kitchen planning. Your theme may be any one of a number of things. But it is necessary. Once you have it, the program begins to take shape.

For example, in that "What's the News" theme, the announcements that go out might suggest the newspaper idea. The moderator might be called "Editor of the Day." The programs might be set in newspaper style. The table decorations might feature flowers in baskets made of newspapers. So on through the entire presentation.

But you and your committee can come up with a much better theme than that!

IF YOU'RE MISTRESS OF CEREMONIES

Know exactly what the program is all about 'and figure in advance how one event can best be tied into the following one. Put all your emphasis on the audience and on the program personnel. You are not there to make an impression for yourself. Look enthusiastic; be enthusiastic. Be complimentary. Your job is to sell the program as it is being presented.

BALANCE YOUR SPEAKERS

Just a word about balancing your speakers. If you ask three or four persons to participate in a program, as in the symposium just described, be sure they are about on a par professionally and about equal in audience appeal. Allot equal time for each talk. Give all the speakers equal amounts of publicity and build-up.

Two speakers on a program are more likely to offer complications than three or four. If you are to have two speakers for a luncheon or evening meeting, you might well make the second feature a demonstration or a brisk report, rather than a conventional speech. An element of this sort makes for variety, yet does not offer competition with the first speaker. Nothing takes the edge off a really good talk more than a second talk which is either a duplication of subject matter or a discussion of something completely extraneous. (If you know that the second speaker might suffer by comparison with the first one, reverse their order of appearance.)

When two speakers of equal importance are to appear, as in a session of a convention, it's a good idea to declare a brief recess between the two talks. At least suggest that the audience stand and stretch before going on with the next phase of the program. Or have the master of ceremonies bridge the gap with a few statements. Each speaker then is queen for her hour. There is no feeling of comparison between the two; no possibility of one's being considered an "A" picture and the other a "B."

It may be your responsibility as a member of a program committee to find the speakers and arrange with them to appear on your program. Your task involves far more than merely extending the invitation. You need to give each prospective speaker a clear word-picture of your group and their interests; explain the theme; state specifically what phase of the discussion you would like her to cover; discuss possible titles that would tie in with the theme. Of course, you must do it all in such a way that she feels complimented.

In many instances it is easier to get one main speaker than it is to get three or four, as for a symposium. Many speakers feel that a 15-minute appearance is scarcely worth the effort of preparation. In such a case you might preface your request with something to the effect that "it takes a really good speaker to do justice to a subject in 15 minutes; that is why our program committee is asking *you* to give one of the three 15-minute talks at our . . ."

In short, when you are involved in the planning of a program, think of it as the editor of a magazine thinks of a forthcoming issue. First he dreams up — i.e., visualizes — what he feels his readers would like to find in the issue. Then he

SCHOOL STYLE SHOWS

Spring brings school style shows in which students proudly display what they have done in sewing. If you are an inexperienced teacher, these themes may suggest something new to do.

Dollar-Sign Show. After a girl has modeled her dress or coat, she picks up a card that tells what the garment cost to make, then, holding card in front of her, models again.

Clothesline Show. All types of clothing made in sewing class are strung on clotheslines at back of stage. Against this gay background, the show goes on.

Suitcase Show. Three or four members of the class unpack suitcases showing clothing made in class. Song and dance numbers are worked in. In one way or another every member of the class gets into the act.

Publicity. All such shows are entitled to publicity. Television is wonderful if it can be arranged to have the show — or at least a part of it — taped.

calls on the best talent possible to bring his dreams to reality. He gives those contributors specific assignments to keep the various features from overlapping. Then he works their contributions together — expanding, cutting, balancing, dramatizing — to produce a unified, streamlined package that will be of interest to every member of his audience. That's exactly what you need to do in putting together a program.

There is, however, one other thing that must be considered. Publicity! Unless the publicity committee can find something on that program which will spark good news stories, there is something wrong with the plan!

Work with your publicity committee from the very start. Try to understand its problems. Perhaps those problems will seem more real to you after you've read the next chapter. It deals with writing publicity for an organization activity, as it relates particularly to promoting a program or a project.

HOME ECONOMICS BLENDING
(An Editorial by G.A.C.)

AS ALL OF US REALIZE, home economics was originally a closely-knit subject, centering around all of the activities of the home. Now it is becoming a profession of specialists. Some of us specialize in foods, some in textiles, in equipment, in child development, or in nutrition, and so on and on.

Question is, even while specializing, is it not possible (and important) for all of us to keep clearly in mind the original over-all concept of our profession? You who are in the teaching field, of course, do that. But some of us who are in business could well give more attention to phases of homemaking outside our own special interest. In other words, emphasize some of the intangibles of good homemaking along with our promotion of tangible products and processes.

Is the program to be printed? Then make it attractive typographically with clean-cut sentences, neat type arrangement. Make it a program that will be kept — not a difficult problem, provided you think of the job as you would a booklet or a piece of advertising copy.

Home economists in the fields of clothing, textiles, and laundering deserve credit for their subtle promotion of personality development, good grooming, and wise money management along with better methods of making and caring for clothing. Perhaps an even better job can be done along that line.

Certainly those of us who work with food products or cooking equipment can punctuate more of our recipes and menus with bits of good information on nutrition or meal management. (Not just for the sake of the product involved, but for the sake of better health and happier cooking!)

Those of us who give demonstrations or prepare educational filmstrips on any subject can work in points that might help build better family relationships. And all of us — teachers and business home economists alike — can do more to educate our particular audiences in the *economics* phase of home economics.

With or without benefit of coordinating committees, each of us can do much to strengthen and vitalize the over-all concept of home economics — and strengthen our individual specialties at the same time.

18.

Organization Publicity

How to find news;
How to report it

WHEN YOU ARE ASKED to take over handling the publicity for your club group or organization, you can do one of two things. You can approach it as a tedious task. Or you can look on it as an opportunity to do something that is exciting and worthwhile.

You choose the challenge route, of course. But again there is that question, how do you proceed? Perhaps you are serving on the publicity committee for the local home economics association. You're urged to "get lots of good publicity" for the organization.

Your first task is to study out what the group is doing or what it can do that is worth telling the public about. An organization publicity story cannot be merely about what the organization *is*. It must tell what the organization *does* — has done, is doing, or is going to do — that will be of real interest to newspaper readers generally. In short, this type of publicity must deal with real *news* if it is to have a chance of being published.

It's the extras you put into a program that make for good publicity regarding it.

Sometimes a meeting that is to be held will provide the needed news element. It will if the speaker is of enough importance locally to make news; if the subject to be discussed or the theme to be followed is of wide and current interest; and if a few intriguing advance quotes from the talk can be given. Mere announcement that such-and-such a group is to hold a meeting at a certain time and place is worthwhile as a reminder to members, of course, but it cannot be considered genuine publicity. Such notices ordinarily go into the club calendar in small type, and that is where they belong.

How To Make News

To work up live, worthwhile publicity for an organization, it is often necessary to *make* news — good news — about the group. Suppose your local home economics association has decided it wants to become a more important factor in the community. It has decided that a consistent publicity campaign will be helpful. How can you hope to get a series of stories about the association into the local papers?

The answer, actually, goes back to the program committee and the program-of-work committee of the organization. It will probably be up to you as publicity chairman to collaborate with these committees. Together you figure out a series of events that will make good news stories which your local papers will be pleased to publish.

Those events might include such standard attractions as a vocational field day for students in local high schools and colleges, with talks by students as well as addresses by leaders in various fields; a joint meeting of the home economics association with the local chapter of architects or decorators; a meeting to be addressed by a well-known physician or psychiatrist; or any one of a

HOW TO INTERVIEW

When you go after a personal interview, phone in advance for an appointment. Never say, "I'd like to get a story." Say, "I'd like to talk with you about . . ." Know in advance what questions you will ask, but don't fire them too fast. Let the conversation develop naturally. Get the other person to talk. Don't hurry. Don't be too obvious about your note taking. And be sure to get the exact spelling of the person's name.

number of other possibilities. Each one of these events would be the basis for a number of newsworthy stories, with plenty of names and plenty of quotable quotes.

Or suppose you're a lunchroom supervisor. You would like to get more parents and other members of the community interested in supporting your school lunch project. How can you manage to get effective publicity about this worthy cause into the local papers?

The answer, again, is *make news* that will make the newspaper columns. You might invite the officers of the school P.T.A. to go through the lines with the youngsters one day, then sit down to lunch with you and discuss your plans and problems. Send an advance story to the club editors of the local papers before the luncheon, and a follow-up report afterward.

Apply that same general plan to the problem of getting publicity for any organization, or for any person. In other words, if there isn't any news, make some that's worth writing about, then write it in a way that's worth reading.

At times it may be advisable for you to take the club editor into your confidence, and tell her enthusiastically about the big program or project that has been scheduled. Invite her to cover the event personally, if she wishes to do so, and write the story as she sees it. Assure her of your complete cooperation. She may decide to get photographs and detailed information in advance so that the feature can appear on the day the event takes place. If this is her preference, work with her, regardless of obstacles.

Writing the News Story

At other times, it may be up to you to write the story. When that is the case, visualize the editor who is to receive your offering. How would she

NEWS STORY PATTERN

When a newspaper reporter writes a simple news item, he follows the pattern of the inverted triangle. That is, he puts all the basic information in the first paragraph, and then adds details in the paragraphs that follow. This makes it easy for a reader to get the gist of the story at a glance; makes it easy for the make-up man to shorten the story by cutting off the bottom paragraphs as needed.

When you write a publicity release or a report of a meeting, follow the same pattern. Put all basic facts in the first paragraph.

like to have it written? The answer is that she wants it written as a news story. And she probably wants to receive it well in advance of the event!

If you have studied newswriting in journalism courses, you know how to proceed. If not, then follow these simple, condensed rules for writing the straight news type of publicity story.

(1) In the very first or lead paragraph pack the most important facts. Make it clear and interesting. Don't let the first paragraph get cumbersome. The reader wants to know: *Who? What? When? Where?*, and sometimes *Why?* and *How?* But the next paragraphs can answer some of these questions. Use some artistry in putting those answers together. Don't begin in that flat, dull, amateurish way, "A meeting was held. . . ."

(2) Give further particulars in the paragraphs that follow. After the most important, most interesting information, give the less important. Remember that the plot plan of a straight news story is an inverted triangle. Arrange your story so that the editor can chop it off at the end of any paragraph without cutting out any main facts.

(3) Follow the typical news style of writing. Keep your paragraphs short. Keep your sentences short and crisp. Keep your entire story short and to the point.

Write in the third person; don't use the words "I," "you," or "we," except when they occur in direct quotations. Be careful to keep all personal opinions out of the story unless they are attributed to a person in direct or indirect quotes.

If you do quote a person, be sure you quote him *accurately*, and be sure you have his approval on your exact wording. Probably more embarrassments are caused by careless quotes than by deliberate misquotes. Never be guilty of either.

PUBLICITY-GRAMS

Avoid meaningless statements in publicity. Talk with editors, get their ideas as to how stories should be handled. Never announce that door prizes or other lottery gifts will be given at a meeting. Newspapers are careful about such statements because of legal restrictions. Send out your releases at sensible intervals. Don't overdo it.

Avoid such terms as *very, interesting,* and, except when necessary, *the following, below, above, the above mentioned, the preceding, the foregoing.* Use of *very* is an indication of verbal poverty.

Tie the story up with names of individuals who are concerned. It's a timeworn but still true maxim that "names make news." When you do use names be absolutely certain that you have every name spelled exactly right, every initial accurate, every firm or organization name, every connection precisely correct. Don't just guess at them; check them. That's what telephones are for.

(4) Put up the story in professional form. That means type it clearly and neatly, double spacing the lines. As a matter of fact, many newspaper editors prefer to have the first paragraph triple spaced, to allow room for editing or rewriting without having to have the story retyped. In general, for your first page follow the layout suggested in the margin, typing the heading down almost in the center of the page, and going on from there.

(5) Find out the name of the person on each local newspaper who should receive your publicity releases. If in doubt as to whether it is the club editor, the women's page editor, the society editor, or the home economics editor who handles such news notes on a certain page, telephone the city desk and inquire. Get the name of the proper editor and send the stories directly to him or her. Be mighty sure you don't make any errors in spelling or initials of *that* name.

State on the copy if the release is exclusive to the particular newspaper, to point out that the story is not being sent to any other paper. In general, it is best to send a semi-exclusive release to each newspaper, using the same facts but different approaches. And, of course, there must be no duplication of photographs.

At this point let's hope that by working enthusiastically with the program committee and the program-of-work committee you have helped generate and publicize an idea that has news

TO SET UP A NEWS RELEASE

In the upper left-hand corner of the page, type your name or the name of your organization. On the next line put the address; next the phone number. On the fourth line give the release date. In the upper right-hand corner, state if release is exclusive. In the middle of the page — about 4 inches down from the top — put the headline. Now write your lead, triple-spacing that paragraph. After the lead, write the rest of the story, double-spacing the copy.

value. It has been given visibility in local papers and over the air. Perhaps, also, in one or more of the neighborhood papers or local magazines. You feel rather proud that you have done a creditable piece of work. But why stop there?

Perhaps that idea, reworked, expanded, and illustrated, might make good reading in the Sunday edition of a state-wide metropolitan newspaper, or be the basis of a story for one of the home economics publications. In either instance, you would, of course, query the editor before submitting the story and photographs.

Don't overlook the possibility of getting publicity (immediately or later) through interviews on local radio and television programs. To do so means working out a just-right air approach and then presenting the idea to the right person. Publicity via air demands that you be enthusiastic — not only about the project itself but about getting the story of it across to the audience.

In your publicity efforts always put on your mental bifocals. Along with looking at the possibilities close at hand, look for others at long range and with wider perspective.

Make no little plans. Put enthusiasm into that publicity job. When you do this, you not only deepen good public relations for your organization, but you broaden your own personal vision and heighten your own visibility as well.

19.

Paper Work

Letters, memos, reports
résumés, and presentations

ALL BUSINESS, professional, and education positions have one thing in common — paper work! There are the never-ending, ever-increasing stacks of letters, memos, and reports to be written; the occasional résumé and presentation. And all of these have one thing in common. They can — and do — help to build good personal, business, public, and professional relations.

This is especially true of the letters that you who are in business write in answer to the inquiries of unknown homemakers. Every time you help one homemaker to solve a problem, you are helping to make several new friends for your department, your company, and your profession.

The same thing happens when you put out a forceful interoffice memo, or send a revealing report to your executives. Through those instruments you help the personnel of your organization to realize what home economics is, and what it can do.

Every time you put up a well-rounded résumé to go with a letter of application, you take a step

The five mirrors that reflect one's personality and abilities.

toward opening the door to new opportunities in home economics.

And many times when you prepare an outstanding presentation of an idea, it proves to be the escalator that carries you to a higher level!

Once you reason in this way, you will certainly be inspired to do a better job of what you have considered routine paper work. Then the question becomes *how*.

Some Definitions

Before going into those "hows," however, some clarification may be in order:

A *letter* is a personalized, personally signed communication from one person to another. Since it is designed to indicate an interest in the person addressed, as well as in the subject matter under discussion, a letter always begins with a personal salutation, as "Dear Mr. _____."

A *memo* is an impersonal note on some one subject to another person or persons. Its one purpose is to suggest an idea or offer a point of view or a recommendation that might benefit the business or organization. Since it is strictly impersonal, no salutation is used. Instead, at the top of the page, some form such as this is employed:

MEMORANDUM

To_____   Subject_____
From_____   Date _____

A *report* goes into details of work done, or progress on an assignment, or aims achieved. Its purpose is to give one's employer or immediate superior or committee chairman a picture of what the writer has been doing. Whether it is set up as a letter or as a memo, the first paragraph should be something of a summary, playing up first the most important thing accomplished. Subsequent paragraphs should then expand and interpret that over-all statement as concisely and clearly as possible.

A *résumé* is a condensed autobiography set down in outline form, as "Education_____. Experience_____, etc." Its purpose is to tell a prospective employer at a glance whether the applicant has qualifications and experience that would make it worthwhile to arrange for an interview.

A *presentation* is a "sales piece." More important and more comprehensive than the usual memo, it is designed not only to sell an idea, but to sell oneself as the person best qualified to put the idea into action.

All such communications should be dated. All should be approached from a positive point of view rather than from a negative one. All should be easy to read, easy to understand.

Five Ways To Improve Your Business Letters

1. Examine a dozen of the letters which you have written during the past few months. As a group are they full of "I," or has the emphasis been put upon the idea and upon the person to whom you are writing? Are the letters brief and brisk almost to the point of curtness? Or do they indicate that, busy though you are, you still take time to be gracious and thoughtful? Are they rambling, confused, inconclusive, full of nothing in particular? Or do they say something and say it clearly and coherently?

Instead of considering how you might have improved some of those letters, stop right now and do a little thinking about yourself. If your letters are spattered with the letter "I," chances are you are thinking too much about yourself and your own problems and affairs. If they sound curt and brusque, perhaps you, under the pressure

DICTAPHONE DETAILS

Know what you are going to say in each letter. Dictate most important ones first, while your mind is fresh. If you are inexperienced, dictate only three or four letters at a sitting, writing each in your mind before you begin. Use a dictaphone occasionally, playing back the records so that you can hear how those letters sound to your secretary.

of business, are getting to be that way. If they are fuzzy and incoherent, it is a sign either that you do not think simply and clearly or that you are careless. Remember, those letters you write are a pretty accurate picture of your own personality. They tell your business contemporaries whether you are friendly, outgoing, and considerate, or self-centered, brusque, and uncooperative.

BUSINESS COURTESY

If you ask a busy person to help you to get a job, courtesy demands that once you have your position, you write immediately to that person to say so and to thank her for her help and interest. If you have been extended any business courtesy while on a trip, those courtesies must be acknowledged soon after you return to your desk.

2. Get the *you* approach into every letter. See that it shows up in the first paragraph — better yet in the first sentence if it seems natural to do so. "You have been in my thoughts a great deal since that conference in San Francisco . . . ." "You are a busy person, but even so I am hoping that you will take time to give me some needed advice. . . ." "At our last meeting you will recall that we discussed such and such." "When I read your letter . . . ."

Putting the emphasis on the one who is being addressed is not a matter of flattery. It is a matter of thoughtfulness. It is business courtesy. And it keeps you from starting out with that unforgivable approach, "I've been too busy, etc." As who hasn't?

3. Make sure that you have answered every question asked in the letter to which you are replying. Anticipate any questions that may occur to him as he reads what you are writing, and answer them in advance.

4. Keep your letters on the affirmative side. Avoid negative statements or implications. Obviously, you will not always agree with others. You cannot always grant requests. But you can phrase your sentences so that a negative thought is expressed affirmatively. Rather than say, "I'm sorry, but I cannot possibly speak to your group next Friday," why not turn the sentence around to say, "I am leaving tonight for Chicago, which means

that it will not be possible for me to meet with your group next Friday, much as I should like to do so."

5. Be sincere. This means that you must be honestly interested in the person to whom you are writing, as well as in what you are writing about. Sincerity, as has been said elsewhere in this book, is something you can't fake. If you have it, it shines through between the lines of everything that you write. If you do not have it, your words do not have it.

Eight Rules for Memo Writing

1. Date every memorandum. Give the name of the person or persons to whom it is being sent. To make it easier to identify and file, and to make it more intelligible, state in the beginning what it is all about.

2. Think of that first paragraph as you would the lead in a news story. Make it a summary of what is in the memo, but do it in a way that will make the reader eager to read all the details that follow. Example: You are a teacher of home economics in a city high school. You are suggesting to the city supervisor that an interschool social event be staged so that all girls taking home economics can become better acquainted and more enthusiastic about home economics. You might approach the memo something like this: "Only 26 girls here at Lincoln High are enrolled in home economics. These girls feel that they are a minority group, and are, I fear, losing interest. The same situation exists in the other city schools. It occurs to me that if we were to get all of our home economics students together for a pleasant social occasion, we might be able to get across some ideas in a way that is not possible in the classroom.

SPECIAL NOTE TO STUDENTS

Writing interesting letters home, going into details of your life at school, is mighty good writing practice. If in spite of all your activities you "can't think of a thing to say," or if you haven't the energy and patience to tell them in a colorful way, how can you ever expect to be a writer?

"As I see it, such an occasion could be handled something like this. . . ."

3. Interpret and elaborate on your statements as necessary in order to bring out the full significance of what you are reporting.

4. Give good *reasons why* whenever you recommend that an idea be carried out. Even though the idea is obviously a good one, point out your reasons, giving evidence to support your statements.

5. Tell how the project or plan can be carried out. Give this information after you have presented your idea and given your reasons why it is, in your opinion, worth adopting or at least exploring. In giving those *hows* include a statement as to how much time and approximately how much money will be required to do the job.

6. Break up long memos typographically to make them look easy to read. Here are some of the ways to do it:

a. Use short paragraphs.

b. Allow extra space between paragraphs.

c. Use subheads when it is feasible to do so.

d. Underscore *key words* or sentences.

e. Indent tabulated statements (just as is done here).

Make it a point to study the memos that come to your desk. Judge them from the standpoint of good or not-so-good typography. Discuss them with your secretary. Just as it is important to be conscious of good layout and type arrangement on a printed page, so is it important to know what constitutes an easy-to-read, well-set-up page of typewritten copy.

7. Keep all subheads parallel in construction. This point in good writing, which has been stressed throughout this book, is equally important in writing all types of memoranda.

MUST YOU CRITICIZE?

If it is absolutely necessary to write a letter of criticism (which it seldom is), begin your letter with a few friendly kind words — a compliment, if possible — then proceed to the less pleasant portion. But, if possible, avoid writing letters of criticism. A personal discussion of the difficulty, either face to face or over long-distance telephone, makes for happier dealings, smoother relationships.

8. Remember, memos that you write tell more than you think they do. They show whether you have ideas and can follow through on them; whether you know what is significant and what is feasible. They reveal your personal traits: whether you look at things negatively or positively; whether you are as eager to give credit to others for their ideas and contributions as you are to get credit for everything that you do. The sum total of the impressions those office communications make often determines the speed at which you are advanced, the extent to which you are given responsibility.

Rules That Apply in Writing Reports

Whatever your position in your organization, routine reports, difficult though they are to write, are one of the important functions of your job. Writing them shows exactly how you have been putting in your time, how you have been spending the company's (or tax-payers' or members') money, what you have been accomplishing. They tell your superiors how you are progressing; give an insight into your work, and into the job itself, that would not otherwise be possible to obtain. They indicate what results may logically be expected in the future. And they give you an opportunity to prove that you are really good.

Your employers may give you something of a pattern to follow in making routine reports. It is not enough, however, merely to fill in that form.

Think through what you have been doing; evaluate it; decide what is significant about it and why. If elasticity is permitted or encouraged — and it usually is — take the time and the space to interpret your findings and observations as suggested in No. 3 under "Rules for Memo Writing."

Interpretation is especially important when fig-

WORKING GUIDE

A book which goes into the specific field of report writing is "Technical and Business Report Preparation" by Robley Winfrey.

Designed primarily to train engineers in the writing of papers and reports, but applicable elsewhere, the book includes instruction in planning reports, the mechanics of style, format, illustrations, correspondence, magazine articles and technical papers, oral reports, letters of application, editing, copyreading and proofreading. "Technical and Business Report Preparation" is published by the Iowa State University Press, Ames, Iowa (1962).

ures are involved. For example, the director of a school cafeteria reports the total amount of money received and paid out for milk. Those financial figures mean little in terms of nutrition or health education unless they are converted first into the number of glasses of milk they represent, then into the number of glasses of milk per child, per day.

Regardless of the form you follow, concentrate first on what you have to say; next on how to say it; and finally, on what you can do to make your copy easy to read and to follow, as suggested in "Rules for Memo Writing." Before final copying is done, check what you have written against this list of questions:

1. Does the title page carry this information: *What* (title of report); *For Whom*; *By Whom*; *Date*? In a several-page report, the title page may well be treated as a cover page, and carry only this information. In a brief report, the information mentioned goes on the first page of the report, above the introduction.

2. Does the title define the subject that is covered in the report?

3. If the report is a long one, is there a table of contents or other outline indicating the order in which topics are discussed? This is not necessary, of course, in the usual interoffice progress or research report. In a several-page report, the outline or table of contents usually follows the cover page.

4. Is there a summary or conclusion? Often this is given in or immediately following the introduction; sometimes it follows the body of the report, before or with the recommendations.

5. Is a distinction made between work done

WHEN YOU ANALYZE CORRESPONDENCE

It's a good idea to have an occasional extra carbon made of letters and put into a folder for special study later. In analyzing them, ask yourself these questions: "Is this letter clear?" "Is it friendly?" "Could it have been written in fewer words?" "How does it look?"

SIMPLE SYSTEM

If the matter of overusing the pronoun *I* confuses you, try this: Don't worry about it — just avoid beginning a paragraph with that perpendicular pronoun.

and objectives accomplished? Between results and conclusions regarding them?

6. Are facts presented in logical order?

7. If references are needed or would prove helpful, are they included? If these are few in number they are usually given as footnotes. If there are a great many they are gathered into a bibliography or appendix at the end of the report.

When your report has been checked against this list, and given its final typing, go over it once more to catch any typographical errors and to see that all figures and data are correct. Then send it along with the same pride you would feel in submitting a story to a magazine.

Suggestions for Writing the Résumé

If you are an about-to-be-graduated home economics student, soon to be looking for a job in teaching or in business, you'll need to prepare a résumé to accompany your letters of application. That résumé will include your background, education, and school activities, plus any other information that might help an employer to get a clear mental picture of you.

In writing, you will have the recommendations of your vocational counselor and your teachers, but it will still be up to you to inject your own personality. If, for example, you worked summers in your father's grocery store or bakery or office, mention that fact. Some employer may be looking for a girl who understands point-of-sale reactions, or who knows office routines. If you are of Italian or French or Spanish or other descent and can write and speak the language, say so. Such information may be of more importance than you realize.

Make sure your résumé is neatly typed and free from spelling errors. Do not send carbon copies

SUCCESSFUL SURVEYS

Ask the right questions. Don't have pre-conceived ideas as to what the survey should show. Remember: "Research must lead; you cannot lead it." Evaluate answers and results honestly. Dramatize results by means of tables and charts to bring them to life, make them understandable.

— they give the wrong impression. With the résumé, send the best letter of application you can possibly write. Then trust that you will find a position that gives you an opportunity to prove what you can do.

If you're an experienced business home economist or teacher or dietitian planning to seek another position, you, too, will write a résumé but your approach will be that of the executive, rather than that of the student. And, like all executives, you will observe these rules:

1. Keep the résumé crisp — not over two pages. Telescope details, but avoid sounding abrupt or curt.

2. List first what you have accomplished most recently, because the top half of that first page is the critical area. From it the executive will decide whether or not to read on. Avoid that tendency to put down facts in chronological order; do include your most noteworthy achievements. If the jobs and years of experience are many, you don't need to be specific about all of the earlier ones!

3. Include a summary of your educational training, plus details of family and community background. Don't hide your age. Many times an employer is looking for a home economist of maturity.

4. Make your accompanying letter of application a sincere statement — not of what you have done (your résumé tells that) but of what you *can* do if you are given a chance at that desired position.

Recommendations for Writing Presentations

There may be times in your career when you will decide to present an important idea or a revo-

TO YOUNG HOME ECONOMISTS

If you are seeking a home economics position in a certain company, do find out whether or not there is an existing home economics department. If there is one, address your letter of application to the home economics director, rather than to the personnel department. It's a more graceful approach.

Find out the initials, name, and title of the proper person in the organization to whom your letter should go. One addressed merely to a firm or organization shows that the writer lacks the "savvy" (or is too lazy) to search out the information.

lutionary plan of work to some firm or organization or foundation. If so, these suggestions may be helpful to you.

1. Think that idea through completely and from all angles before you attempt a written presentation. Make sure you have something really important to offer, and that the plan is workable.

2. Plan to send a short note or letter along with the presentation. That letter will serve as the door opener to the idea. Then you can devote all the presentation to the idea itself and to how it can be carried out.

3. State exactly, in the first paragraph, what the idea is about. Then in subsequent paragraphs explore, expand, and explain the idea, and point out briefly a plan of work.

4. Pave the way for a personal interview to discuss that plan of work further, rather than write down details to the point of monotony. The reasoning here is to leave the door open until your presentation has been accepted or rejected.

5. Remember that it is difficult to "sell" an idea unless you sell a plan of work, and sell yourself as the person to carry it out. Few companies have budgets that permit them to buy contributions (as such) from outside the company. But you can hope to get the assignment to follow through, perhaps on a consultant basis.

6. Give importance to your carefully thought out, carefully typed presentation. Put it into a folder or between covers. If it's a long presentation, state near the beginning that the information has been broken down into four or five parts to make for easier reading. Then state what those parts are — let it be a miniature index or table of contents for your piece.

**FORMS OF COMPLI-
MENTARY CLOSE**

Businesswomen usually close their letters with "Very sincerely yours," or "Sincerely yours." "Sincerely" is used in letters of friendship. Forms of "truly" are considered more formal, less warm.

TO FOLD A LETTER

For a small envelope: Bring the lower edge of the 8 x 11-inch sheet up to about ½ inch from top and crease. Then fold from right to left a little more than ⅓ the width of the sheet. Then fold from left to right and crease again so it opens like a book.

For a long envelope: Fold a little less than a third of the sheet from bottom toward top and crease. Then fold upward to within ½ inch of top and crease again.

Don't be guilty of using incorrect postage. Write the Post Office Department, Washington 25, D. C., for "Domestic Postage Rates." Free.

SPEAKING OF WORDS, isn't it significant that "home," one of the most meaningful words in our language, is the root word of home economics? Isn't it exciting to know that ours is the one recognized profession in which the word "home" appears? It gives us pause, however, to realize that, because of this unique fact, it is our responsibility to safeguard that word "home"; to make sure that its true meaning is neither diluted nor devaluated.

It is not easy to live up to that responsibility. There is often the pressure (or the inclination) to stress frills of homemaking above fundamentals. A temptation to teach or preach "do this, do that," rather than to reach out to where the homemaker lives and inspire her to better ways of living as well as doing. A danger of becoming blinded not only by the glitter of non-essentials, but also by the glittering generalities that are so likely to cloud our communications!

But our work is cut out for us. Acknowledging that homemaking is changing, and that we must change some of our approaches to it, our job is — and must be — to keep the home in Home Economics. — G.A.C.

20.

Copy Editing and Proofreading

How to follow through
on a piece of writing

IN MAKING FLOUR INTO BREAD, the dough must be kneaded and turned, pulled and punched, set aside, then kneaded again before it can be shaped into loaves for baking.

The same is true of writing. After the copy has been put into what seems finished form, it must be worked and reworked before it is shaped into final form for the printer. In other words, it must be edited.

Too many persons think of editing as putting in commas, changing words here and there. Such correction of punctuation, spelling, and construction is merely checking. It is important, of course, but true editing goes far beyond such routines. Whether you are editing something that you yourself have written, or going over copy written by someone else, approach the job in this way.

Analyze the Copy as a Whole

Read the copy through. But leave your pencil on the desk during the first reading. You don't need one yet. That first reading is to give you

Copy editing is like the final pressing you give a garment when you have finished it.

an over-all picture of what the copy is about. As you read, keep asking yourself these questions: What is this copy trying to say? Does the information come through? Does the copy answer all of the questions that the reader is likely to ask of it? Are there any important facts omitted?

At this point pick up your pencil and, in the margin of the copy, make note of any details that should be included to round out that information.

Visualize Readers, Visualize Format

Ask, "Who is to read this? Will those readers understand it, be interested in it?" An article on some phase of nutrition research written for publication in a scientific journal, entirely understandable to the professional women reading it, would probably be just so much Greek to nonprofessional homemakers. Know how and where a piece of copy is to be used. Visualize that audience of readers, then go through the copy and ring every word that might not be clear to that particular group.

Visualize, too, the space that probably will be allowed for the copy. If the writer has turned in a 3,500 word story for a magazine which uses no articles longer than 1,200 words, the material will ordinarily have to be rewritten rather than merely edited or cut.

Organize and Scrutinize

Having analyzed and visualized, you are ready to examine the copy from the standpoint of organization. In doing this, consider these points:

1. Are these directions — or this information — given in orderly progression?

2. Does the material keep to one point of view? When allowable shifts in point of view occur, are

WHEN TABULATING FIGURES

In setting up tables of figures, remember: If there are only two columns of figures, no vertical dividing lines are necessary. If there are three or more columns, use perpendicular lines to separate the figures.

ECONOMY NOTE

All errors discovered in reading proof must, of course, be corrected even though the copy is ready to go to press. It should be remembered, however, that typographical changes cost money. If you prepare your copy thoughtfully, and if you read the galley proofs with care, such changes will not ordinarily be necessary.

they handled well by beginning a new paragraph or using parentheses? If not, correct them.

3. If subheads are used, are they parallel in construction?

4. Is the wording consistent throughout? (Not "teaspoons" in one paragraph, "tsps." in another.) If copy is not consistent, make it so.

5. Is the copy loose and wordy, stilted and old-fashioned sounding? Ruthlessly weed out all meaningless phrases, sentences, and paragraphs which add neither information nor interest.

Step Up Dramatization

Look for all possible ways to give the copy more life. Begin with the title. Can you think of a better one? Does the lead carry the reader right into the copy or off in a different direction? Is it short and to the point? One magazine editor says: "The lead paragraph of a magazine article should rarely be longer than 40 words."

Study the sentences. Shorten the over-long ones. Sentences should not be all the same length, but the average length should be kept to 18 words, if possible. Much depends, of course, on how and where the copy is to be used. Sentences in books can be longer than sentences in newspapers. Sentences in a magazine article directed to professional people can be more involved than sentences written for the general public.

Break down over-long paragraphs, too. A few magazine editors insist on keeping paragraphs to not more than 100 words. All such shortening and tightening is definitely a part of good editing.

Check copy for weak words. Substitute more precise ones, more colorful ones, wherever empty words occur. Weed out practically all of those *very's* and as many *the's* and *a's* as you can spare. Scrutinize each adjective. Is it needed? (Remem-

DESK EQUIPMENT

The well-equipped desk for a home economist includes not only standard reference books in her particular field, but a standard dictionary, a desk style book, and a book or booklet showing type faces and sizes. A desk dictionary devotes several pages to Preparation of Copy for the Press.

OLD RULE

Write spontaneously; revise impersonally.

MARK THAT COPY

Before releasing a piece of copy to a printer be sure that it is marked to show what face and size of type are to be used; what width the copy is to be set.

ber that journalistic saying, "The adjective is the enemy of the noun!")

This phase of your editing is a combination of cutting out and putting in. It is the final touch that puts the punch into what you have written. After you have done all of this, the copy will need to be retyped, then checked again for misspelled words and slip-ups in punctuation. Before releasing the copy give it a final look-over to see that you have improved it, not merely made changes. Make sure you have not altered the meaning, but, instead, have made it more clear. Above all, make certain that you have not killed the yeast of spontaneity and enthusiasm.

Yes, editing a piece of copy, like kneading bread, takes energy as well as know-how. It is hard work. But when the copy, like the bread, comes out fresh and light yet full of substance, you feel a deep sense of satisfaction that comes of useful work well done.

Read Proof Pages with Utmost Care

Once a piece of writing is undertaken, there seems to be no end to the work that must be done on it. Even after it has been set in type, it must be proofread — not once but several times and by several persons.

When galleys or page proofs come to your desk, check them carefully against the originals to see that no ingredients have been dropped from those recipes and that there are no omissions or errors. If the copy involves figures, make sure they are absolutely correct. Your job is to see that the copy is right from the standpoint of sense and that no typographical errors have been overlooked by the printer's proofreaders.

In order to catch all inaccuracies, it's a good idea to read the proofs through silently, concen-

TYPOGRAPHICAL WIDOWS

"Widow" is an old-time printing term for a word or part-word that dangles in a separate line at the end of a paragraph. Such fringes are unattractive, especially when they occur at the bottom of a caption or a page. It is usually advisable to cut back a word or two within the last sentence in order to eliminate this over-hang.

PAGE PROOFS

In reading page proofs, note balance of type with white space. If a paragraph of copy looks crowded, while there is much white space at top or bottom of the paragraph, ask the printer to put a 1- or 2-point lead between the lines. (Better yet, ask his advice about doing so — he may have a better suggestion.)

trating on what the copy says, how the individual words look. Then check them again while another person reads aloud from the original manuscript. Take special note of headings and captions; it's doubly easy, it seems, to let an error slip past in these obvious spots. Read syllable by syllable. Don't anticipate how a word will be spelled. Make sure it *is* that way.

Watch for the printer's notations. Often the printer will question a statement or a word. Check it, he's probably right! In marking corrections on proofs, use standard proofreader's marks. (See pages 174 to 176 for editing and copyreading symbols, and proofreading symbols.)

Write all corrections in margins — never between lines. When you have read and marked a galley or a page proof, initial it. If there are no corrections to be made, mark the page "O.K." with your initials following, or "O.K. as corrected," if there are only one or two minor corrections to be made. If you initial copy without marking it O.K. it indicates to the printer or compositor that another proof is expected.

When proofs are delivered to you for correction, the original manuscript will probably be enclosed with them. Be sure to send this manuscript back when you send the corrected proofs. Read and return proofs promptly, but take whatever time is needed to do the job thoroughly and accurately. Don't let yourself be hurried.

Make sure the copy is absolutely right before you finally O.K. it, but keep in mind that revisions cost money. Don't permit yourself to get "finicky" after the copy has all been set. Above all else, remember that once that copy comes off the press, there is no recalling it, no chance for further correction or explanation!

(See next pages for copyreading and proofreading symbols.)

REMEMBER

When proofreading, it's a good idea to use a sheet of unruled paper. Lay it over the copy so that it comes just below the line you are reading. This keeps your eyes on the line that you are reading, makes it easier to see errors.

If in spite of all your carefulness your copy comes out with an error in it, be disturbed. Yes. But don't be upset. Just be more careful another time. "Look out, not in; ahead, not back," is an old standby rule for all who write.

COPYREADING SYMBOLS

	HOW THEY ARE USED	WHAT THEY MEAN	HOW TYPE IS SET
TYPE SIZE and STYLE	Lansing, mich.--	Capitalize.	LANSING, Mich.—
	College Herald	Small caps.	COLLEGE HERALD
	the Senator from Ohio	Change to lower case.	the senator from Ohio
	By Alvin Jones	Bold face.	**By Alvin Jones**
	Saturday Evening Post	Italicize.	*Saturday Evening Post*
PUNCTUATION and SPELLING	"The Spy"	Emphasize quotes.	"The Spy"
	Northwestern U.	Emphasize periods.	Northwestern U.
	said "I must . . .	Emphasize comma.	said, "I must . . .
	Johnsons'	Emphasize apostrophe.	Johnsons'
	picnicing	Insert letter or word.	picnicking
	theatre	Transpose letters.	theater
	Henry Cook, principal	Transpose words.	Principal Henry Cook
	days	Delete letter.	day
	judgement	Delete letter and bridge over.	judgment
	all right	Insert space.	all right
	those	Close up space.	those
	Geo. Brown	Spell out.	George Brown
	100 or more	Spell out.	one hundred or more
	Doctor S. E. Smith	Abbreviate.	Dr. S. E. Smith
	Six North Street	Use numerals.	6 North Street
	Marion Smythe	Spell as written.	Marion Smythe
POSITION	Madison, Wis.--	Indent for paragraph.	Madison, Wis.—
	today. Tomorrow he	New paragraph.	today. Tomorrow he
	considered serious. Visitors are not	No paragraph. Run in with preceding matter.	considered serious. Visitors are not
	But he called last night and said that he	No paragraph.	But he called last night and said that he
	]Jones To Conduct[or <Jones To Conduct>	Center subheads.	**Jones To Conduct**
MISCELLANEOUS	He was not unmindful	Bridge over material omitted.	He was mindful
	one student came	Kill corrections.	one student came
	or more	Story unfinished.	
	30 or #	End of story.	————

By permission from *Scholastic Journalism*, Earl English and Clarence Hach, © Iowa State University Press.

PROOFREADING SYMBOLS

	SYMBOL	EXPLANATION	EXAMPLE: MARGINAL MARKS	EXAMPLE: ERRORS MARKED
TYPE SIZE and STYLE	*wf*	Wrong font.	*wf*	He marked the proof.
	×	Burred or broken letter. Clean or replace.	×	He marked the proof.
	ital	Reset in italic type the matter indicated.	*ital*	He marked the proof.
	rom	Reset in roman (regular) type, matter indicated.	*rom*	He marked *the* proof.
	bf	Reset in bold face type, word or words indicated.	*bf*	He marked the proof.
	≡	Replace with a capital the letter indicated.	*H* ≡	he marked the proof.
	lc	Set in lower case type.	*lc*	He Marked the proof.
	sc	Use small capitals instead of the type now used.	*sc*	He marked the proof.
	9	Turn inverted letter indicated.	9	He ma ked the proof.
PUNCTUATION and SPELLING	∂	Take out letter, letters, or words indicated.	∂	He marked the proof.
	#	Insert space where indicated.	#	He marked theproof.
	r	Insert letter as indicated.	*r*	He maked the proof.
	⊙	Insert period where indicated.	⊙	He marked the proof
	,/	Insert comma where indicated.	,/	Yes he marked the proof.
	’	Insert apostrophe where indicated.	’	Mark the boys proof.
	/=/	Insert hyphen where indicated.	/=/	It was a cureall.
	?/	Insert question mark where indicated.	?/	Who marked the proof
	em	Insert em dash, implying break in continuity or sentence structure.	*em*	Should we can we comply?
	en	Insert en dash, implying the word "to."	*en*	See pages 278 93.
	“ / ”	Enclose in quotation marks as indicated.	“ / ”	He marked it proof.
	spell out	Spell out all words marked with a circle.	*spell out*	He marked the 2nd proof.
	out, see copy	Used when words left out are to be set from copy and inserted as indicated.	*out, see copy*	He proof.
	stet. . .	Let it stand. Disregard all marks above the dots.	*stet*	He ~~marked~~ the proof.
	⁀	Draw the word together.	⁀	He ma rked the proof.
	tr	Transpose letters or words as indicated.	*tr*	He the proof marked
	(?)	Query to author. Encircled in red.	*? was*	The proof read by
POSITION	¶	Start a new paragraph as indicated.	¶	reading The boy marked
	No ¶	Should not be a separate paragraph. Run in.	*No* ¶	marked. The proof was read by
	=	Out of alignment. Straighten.	=	He marked the proof.
	□	Indent 1 em.	□	He marked the proof.
	□□	Indent 2 ems.	□□	He marked the proof.
	□□□	Indent 3 ems.	□□□	He marked the proof.
	eq.#	Equalize spacing.	*eq.#*	He marked the proof.
	⊥	Push down space which is showing up.	⊥	He marked the proof.
	[or]	Move over to the point indicated. [If to the left; if to the right]	[	[He marked the proof.
	⊔	Lower to the point indicated.	⊔	He marked the proof.
	⊓	Raise to the point indicated.	⊓	He marked the proof.
	◡	Less space.	◡	looks better

By permission from *Scholastic Journalism*, Earl English and Clarence Hach,
© Iowa State University Press.

DECLARATION OF INDEPENDENCE

When, in the Course of human events, it becomes nec-
cessary for one people to dissolve the Political bands
which have connected them with another, and to
assume among those powers of the Earth, the eparate
and equal station which to the Laws of Nature and of
Nature God entitle them, a decent re spect to the
opinions of mankind requires that they should declare
the cases which impel them to the sparation.
We hold these truths to be self-evident, that all men
are created equal, that they are endowed by their creator
with certain unalienable Rights, that among these are
Life, Liberty and the persuit of happiness. That to se-
cure these rights, Governments, are instituted among
Men, deriving their just powers from the consent of the
governed. That whenever ny form of government becomes destructive to these ends, it is the Right of the

These sample paragraphs show two different ways of marking
proof. The first method is used by many printing houses because it
is simpler and quicker. The general rule is: Draw your leader line
up into the nearest white space — either margin.

In the second method, a carat is inserted wherever a correction
is necessary. Proofreading symbol is shown in the margin level with
the line to be corrected.

Declaration of Independence

When, in the Course of human events, it becomes necessary for one people to dissolve the Political bands
which have connected them with another, and to
assume among those powers of the Earth, the eparate
and equal station which to the Laws of Nature and of
Nature God entitle them, a decent re spect to the
opinions of mankind requires that they should declare
the cases which impel them to the sparation.
We hold these truths to be self-evident, that all men
are created equal, that they are endowed by their creator
with certain unalienable Rights, that among these are
Life, Liberty and the persuit of happiness. That to se-
cure these rights, Governments/ are instituted among
Men, deriving their just powers from the consent of the
governed. That whenever ny form of government becomes destructive to these ends, it is the Right of the

21.

Food Photogenics

Techniques that make
for better pictures

IN EACH of the Workshops in Home Economics Writing which we (R/C) have conducted in 44 cities from the Pacific to the Atlantic, an open discussion of the problems of handling individual foods for editorial photographs has been a highlight. Home economists everywhere have been most generous in sharing their experiences, passing along their findings.

Here are some of the notes gathered in those meetings. They are not to be taken as the last word in handling foods for photographing. (After all, every photograph is an experiment!) They are put down here for the special benefit of amateurs in this fascinating field. If you are experienced, you have probably worked out your own solutions to these problems — better ones, perhaps, than some of those that follow. In any case, you may like to use these margins for your photographic notes. — G.A.C.

*The secret of good facial make-up
is to heighten natural beauty.
The same is true in
handling foods for photographing.*

Appetizers. Don't try to show a great variety of canapés on one plate. Narrow your choice to a few kinds, then arrange groupings of each kind to make a pleasing over-all design. Select types that have definite form — crackers, shrimp, miniature sausages, olives, for example.

If you are to show a bowl of dip or dunk, break up its flat surface with a few definite dashes of chopped parsley, a few bits of pimiento, or some chopped walnuts or toasted almonds — whatever is appropriate.

When illustrating a canapé spread, give it form by heaping it in a bowl or on a plate or shaping it into a mound or loaf. Then garnish it lightly.

If you're using potato or corn chips, place them in position one at a time. Use perfect ones — some light colored, some darker — so there will be a good definition between them.

Bacon. If rather flat, lightly crinkled bacon is wanted, lay the slices on a rack and put another rack on top. Then bake in moderately hot oven.

More often, art directors ask for bacon slices with a definite ripple or wave. To achieve this, shape a strip of doubled foil the size of the slice. Lay the bacon on it, then "flute" foil-and-bacon over fingers to make deep ripples. Arrange in shallow pan, set on lowest oven rack under broiler, and cook just until clear and glistening.

Individual baked products are discussed in alphabetical order. (See Biscuits, Breads, Cakes, etc.)

Baked Products. Baking for pictures is an important part of the responsibilities of hundreds of home economists. As one department head expressed it, "You can't sell a picture of flour — but a picture of a luscious cake can sell flour!"

To bake photogenic breads, cakes, pies, cookies, etc., the amateur must know what constitutes a perfect product in each category, and must have the skill to turn out a top-quality product.

Ability to recognize the characteristics of a perfect product comes from education and constant observation and awareness. Ability to produce a perfect product comes from practice, study, experimentation — and more practice.

Biscuits. To turn out photogenic biscuits — tall, flaky ones with straight sides and level tops, not lopsided and uneven — expert home economists roll the dough between two guide-bars of proper thickness, usually ½ inch. The rolling pin, of course, rolls on the guide bars.

To cut out biscuits with straight, true sides, place the floured cutter carefully upright on the dough, then press straight down with even pressure. (Don't twist the cutter.) Don't cut biscuits close together — leave an inch or more of dough between them as you cut. You will probably have to mix, roll, cut, and bake several batches in order to get a dozen perfect biscuits for the picture!

How deeply browned should the biscuits be? Usually a normally rich, golden brown is right for either color or black and white photograph. In case of doubt ask the photographer.

Barbecuing. Outdoor atmosphere can be provided or at least suggested in studio. Have steaks or chops cut extra thick. If real charcoal fire is used in grill, blow or knock thick gray ash off coals just before shooting. (A vacuum cleaner tube in reverse works fine, making coals glow brightly, and providing a bit of smoke for extra atmosphere.) Broil the meat in range, ready to transfer to grill at proper moment. Use a heated skewer to make needed grill marks. If fake coals have to be used, sift ashes over them for realism.

Breads. Exterior shape, proportions, and color, and interior texture are of top importance. For nut breads and the like, loaf pans somewhat smaller, deeper, and narrower than standard 9"x5"x3" are often a good choice. Since such breads are usually shown cut, good distribution of nuts and fruit is a problem. (Solution: have several loaves on hand.) Don't worry about a crack in the top of a loaf of quick bread; it is characteristic. But do consider adding interest to that top crust before or after baking — with big pieces of nuts or fruit, perhaps; or a sparkling sprinkling of sugar and cinnamon; or a simple powdered sugar glaze after baking.

Beer. Have several glasses or mugs chilled — near zero if possible — to assure frosting just right. Pour beer from a little height, to insure deep head of foam. Same method applies to root beer.

Butter or Margarine. Cutting a perfect slice is not easy — but some types of cheese slicers with wire for blade do a good job. To keep butter from melting under the lights, freeze it with dry ice and have plate very cold. If necessary, use dry ice under the plate. For use on pancakes: if the cakes are hot there's no problem. If they are cold, a hot knife, or a light held close above the butter will melt it just right.

Cakes. Make layers, loaves, or sheets somewhat thicker and higher than usual, or they are likely to appear thin and flat in finished picture. Experiment in advance to discover the just-right thickness for cake to fit a special layout. Most cakes are shown cut, to add interest and to show color and texture of cake itself. Fancy-shaped ones, however, such as heart, star, etc., are best left uncut to avoid destroying the design.

To cut cake. Good texture of the cut surface depends a great deal on the knife and the handling of it. Use a sharp, thin-bladed knife. (Some experts prefer a bread knife with fine, even serrations.) Saw gently up-and-down — don't press! This knife technique roughs up the surface and makes the crumb look fluffy and velvety, not hard and dry. To emphasize velvetiness (especially for television), go over surface gently with a toothpick, lifting tiny crumbs so they will catch the light.

To cut a frosted cake. Insert knife straight down in center of cake, and saw lightly with up-and-down motion, in order not to drag frosting down onto cut surface of cake. After taking out pieces, use toothpick or tip of knife to remove frosting that does show on the crumb. (Chocolate frosting on light cake causes the biggest problem.)

To cut a sheet cake. Follow directions given for cutting candy and bar cookies. Freezing or chilling the cake helps in cutting neat, sharp-edged shapes for *petits fours.*

Candy. Make fudge and the like extra-deep in pan, so layer will not look thin. Use large pieces of nuts or fruits, whole cherries, etc., so they will show up well.

To cut candy in even squares or bars. Turn it out of pan onto cutting board, if practicable. Measure and mark lines for cutting, using toothpicks. Then, using long, sharp chef's knife, press straight down to make sharp, clean edges.

Canning. Barely heat the fruit or vegetables before packing in jars, or they will look over-cooked. Use clear or light-colored pickling syrup on fruits. Strain syrup so it won't look cloudy.

Casseroles and Mixtures. Use a light hand in putting mixtures together, whether to be shown in a casserole or bowl or on a platter. Keep ingredients in recognizable pieces so far as possible, and arrange to have some of them show up in the top layer. Figure some sort of design or garnish to break up flat expanse of top and to add interest. Perhaps cheese strips or triangles, or drifts of shredded cheese; green or red pepper rings; onion rings; sliced or quartered hard-cooked eggs; sprigs of parsley, or dashes of chopped parsley, etc.

Cereals. For most purposes, care in handling and speed in shooting are all that are needed. For some very special shots, a photographer may air-brush cereal flakes with paraffin to keep them from softening too quickly when milk is poured on.

Cottage Cheese. To bring out its texture, rinse most of the cottage cheese in cold water, drain well, then mix lightly with a little of the undrained so that it looks natural and moist but not "soupy." Tint the undrained cheese delicately with yellow food color or black dye. Dead white foods are inclined to come out looking like blank spots in a printed photograph, whether in color or in black and white.

To avoid a flat look, heap the cottage cheese in a mound. Break up a large expanse of white by adroit use of a fruit or vegetable garnish or dressing.

PICTURE PUZZLE

Have you ever said, "I wonder just what recipe and which pans we used for the cake in this picture?" To avoid such wondering it pays to keep special notebooks or files, complete with print or proof of each picture used in publicity or advertising. To each attach notes as to recipes, pan sizes, weights of batter per pan, kind of frosting used — all the data you might need if you were asked to do a new setup of the same subject.

Chicken (Broiled or Fried). Pull skin over ends of thighs, drumsticks, etc., and sew or pin in place so it won't shrink while cooking. Pin skin to bone at small end of leg. Cook some pieces light brown, some darker, to provide contrast on platter. Don't overcook or it will look dry.

If rosy tone is desired for fried chicken, mix paprika with flour used for coating.

Chocolate. Generally speaking, keep chocolate frostings, cakes, etc., fairly light brown in color. Dark browns come out darker yet in printing, whether in color or in black and white.

Coconut. Flaked coconut, lightly pressed into or drifted over frosting, etc., gives a good effect. A fluffy texture is the aim.

Coffee. The real thing can't be improved upon, though brown dye can be used. For that "freshly poured" look, float a few small bubbles on coffee in the cup. (To make bubbles, stir a little liquid detergent and coffee together in separate cup.)

Cookies. Choose display plate or tray in proportion to size of cookies, and of color and texture to give good contrast. If they are to be topped with almonds, walnut halves, raisins, etc., make the cookies in good proportion to the trimming. (A huge cooky will dwarf a walnut half.)

If just one kind of cooky is to be shown on a plate, bake some fairly light, some darker, to permit choice under the camera lens, and to insure contrast and separation between overlapping cookies. If two or more kinds are to be shown, arrange them in groupings — e.g., chocolate drop cookies in one group, frosted sugar cookies in another. Choose types that have contrast yet go well together. And don't try to show too many varieties on one plate! By the way, wire cooling racks often are more effective for displaying cookies than the usual plate or tray.

One of the big problems in planning a photograph of cookies is to keep them from looking too flat.

Composition of the picture and camera angle can do a lot to provide height. Sometimes a two-tier or three-tier plate is used to display the cookies. A well-designed cooky jar can do a lot for a picture. One that is too cute or coy is better omitted.

To cut bar cookies. See "Candy." Same directions apply here.

Cream, Whipped. Secret of whipping cream so it will hold up beautifully without weeping is simple. Before whipping, add 3 tablespoons powdered sugar for each half-pint of chilled cream. (A few drops of yellow food color may be needed for color photography, or a little black dye for black and white. See "Cottage Cheese.") Whip stiff. Lift whipped cream lightly with spoon for toppings, or put through pastry tube.

In an emergency, shaving cream lather can be used, but real whipped cream is much to be preferred.

EGGS. These innocent-seeming objects can present a variety of difficulties. Whatever way they are to be cooked, Rule Number One is to have dozens of eggs at hand.

Hard-cooked Eggs. Turning carton of eggs upside down in refrigerator the day before cooking, helps (sometimes) to keep yolks centered. To reduce chances of dark ring around yolk, cook 30 minutes in water just below boiling point (around 185°), then cool quickly under running cold water. At once crackle shell finely all over by rolling egg under palm of hand against sink or table, so membrane and shell will slip off easily and smoothly.

Why do some hard-cooked eggs refuse to peel smoothly? Because they are too fresh! Solution suggested by researchers: keep eggs in refrigerator for a week, or let them stand at ordinary room temperature for a day to "age" them slightly before cooking. Some home economists report that it helps also to start the eggs in warm water, heat to boiling, then immediately turn down heat and let them simmer 18 to 25 minutes (depending on size of eggs).

ANOTHER CREAM TRICK

Whip cream 2 hours ahead of using. When ready to use, fold in a little unwhipped cream to give a soft, natural appearance.

EGGS

To keep shelled hard-cooked eggs perfect in shape, float them in ice water in the refrigerator.

Fried Eggs. Here are three ways that various home economists find workable for frying eggs for pictures.

1. Have plenty of oil or strained bacon drippings moderately hot in skillet. If a single egg, round in shape, is needed, set a muffin ring (or a tuna can with both ends cut out) in the hot fat. After sliding the egg into the ring, use your finger or a knife handle to hold yolk centered. Just before white is "set" around edges, lift ring and let white flow so it will look natural. Cook very slowly — about 8 to 10 minutes. When white is set, lift egg carefully into a shallow bowl containing enough mineral oil to cover it completely to keep top from drying.

2. Sometimes a fried egg (or two eggs) must be shaped in a particular way to fit in nicely with other foods on the plate. To do this, cut a cardboard pattern the exact size and shape desired. Set pattern on foil, turn up edges of foil around it, then trim off, making a sturdy rim ½-inch high. Remove cardboard. Put foil "pan" into skillet, with plenty of oil in and around the foil. Slip in the egg or eggs and cook very slowly, holding yolks in place with fingers or with the side of a fork. When white is set, immerse egg in mineral oil as suggested under "1."

3. Occasionally an egg has to be "assembled" for a picture. Two raw egg whites are combined and fried as one by the first method suggested. Then a neat round depression is scooped out of the cooked white, and a raw yolk is dropped in just before the camera clicks.

Scrambled Eggs. Beat them very slightly, so that good flecks of white will show up in the yellow mass. Have them just firm enough to mound nicely. Figure out a way to "contain" them on the plate; perhaps heaped in a toast cup, or bounded by sausages or bacon, or — well, that's your job to think up answers to such problems!

Fish and Seafood. Trout, shrimp, lobster, and some other seafoods have definite form, and so make fairly easy subjects for photographing. For canned tuna, salmon, and the like, form and interest must usually be provided by the way the product is prepared and served. For example, a fish or seafood salad may be simply packed into a fish-shaped mold, turned out on a platter and appropriately garnished. Or it may be — and often is — presented in a fish-shaped bowl or plate. Or a fish cut out of pastry or carrot (for goldfish!) or other amusing garnish may be used to say "fish."

In making up a casserole or creamed dish featuring tuna or salmon it is important to use big, recognizable chunks or flakes and arrange them so that they really show up. Reason for this exaggeration is that so much detail is lost in reproduction.

Handling of these foods under lights deserves some mention. Shrimp fades, and usually has to be touched up with food color. Canned tuna dries and changes color quickly when exposed to air. Photogenic chunks and pieces selected from freshly opened cans may be covered with mineral oil to keep them in good condition, ready to replace faded "stand-ins" just before shooting.

Frankfurters and Sausages. These have definite and interesting form. Hence on a plate or platter they combine well with foods of softer texture and less dominant shape to make a good design. A neat mound of salad, for instance, or scrambled eggs.

Grilled franks may shrivel or wrinkle a bit as they cool while being arranged under the camera. They can be replumped by dropping into boiling water for a minute or so, then brushed with oil and photographed immediately.

Frostings. Unless the frosting you plan to use will hold up well under hot lights, be sure to have a stand-in cake frosted the same way. In putting a layer cake together for a picture, don't be too generous with soft frosting between the layers, or it is likely to bulge out and show as a ridge around the sides of the finished cake. After putting layers together with frosting or filling, wait a few minutes for this to "set" before frosting top and sides. Do frost top and sides lavishly, with fairly deep swirls or markings so that lights and shadows may give it interesting "modeling." But avoid a too-labored look.

FROSTINGS

Angel food or sponge cake turned out on a plate is likely to show an uneven edge against the plate, which may present a problem in frosting the cake. Solution: using a pastry tube or paper cone, fill in those open spaces with frosting and let stand until firm before frosting the cake. (Small holes in the surface of the cake can also be filled in by this system.)

Be sure to make plenty of frosting all at once — or make two or three batches and mix them. Trying to match one batch of frosting with another in color and texture can be as frustrating as trying to mix paint to match what has been spread!

In making Seven-Minute Frosting for photographic use, it is advisable to beat it a shorter time than usual. It will stay more pliable, and can be re-worked on the cake if necessary. This type of frosting, being snowy white, tints nicely.

Labor-saving note: Styrofoam "cakes," cut in desired shapes and sizes, work well for frosting displays, and can be used for pictures where the cakes are not to be cut. The frosting can be washed off and the cakes reused indefinitely.

FOIL

Are there times when you need to use household foil in your photographic setup? Then follow the advice of experts and wear gloves so that fingerprints do not show. (One photographer wears the type of gloves worn by pall-bearers!)

FRUITS. Handle as little as possible. Use pieces large enough to be recognizable, keeping natural form insofar as feasible. To prevent discoloration of raw pieces, dip in lemon juice or anti-oxidant solution. Cook fruits very lightly; handle gently; coat with syrup for gloss.

Apples, Baked. Don't core them all the way through — just the top. Good natural effect can be achieved by cooking apples in plenty of medium syrup on top of range, turning often, until they look soft on outside. Then finish as desired in hot oven or under broiler, watching constantly.

Avocados. These must be ripe enough so skin can be stripped off. (Never pare an avocado with a knife!) Cut in halves first, remove seed, then handle from inside while peeling, slicing, and arranging. Don't touch the fragile, smooth green surface with a brush — pour lemon juice over all and use finger tips as applicators. When mashed avocado is to be shown, add a little pale green color; otherwise it looks yellow and unrecognizable.

Bananas. Uncluttered design in arrangement of salads, etc., is a must for these and many other fruits. Use lettuce sparingly.

Berries. Like beets, most red berries tend to look purplish in color photographs, black in black and white photographs. The photographer's advice is best to follow. But take plenty of berries from which to choose perfect individual ones.

Cherries. Need a few Maraschino cherries? Look for brands with brightest, clearest red. (Consider other ways, too, of putting needed touches of red into color photos — red jelly, for example.)

Cherries for Pie. Some use Maraschino cherries, soaking them to remove some of the redness. Easier way is to drain canned Royal Anne (white) cherries, then dye them to the desired shade of red with food color. (Don't pit them.)

Cranberries. Cook lightly, to keep bright color. For cranberry jelly, dilute juice slightly with water and use gelatin. Slice canned cranberry sauce so that surface looks "rippled," not solid and hard. A slightly crumpled piece of white paper under a slice sometimes helps to let light through.

Fruit Cocktail. Assemble your own, in order to have pieces with sharply cut edges and good form. (Open a can of fruit cocktail for a guide, and a can of each type of fruit used in it. Cut these fruits in same size and shape as original, and combine in same proportions. Use thin, clear syrup on them.

Olives, Green or Stuffed. Look for best color. Choose size in good proportion to other items. If to be cut, use thick slices or wedges, and arrange so they look casual.

Olives, Ripe. Drain and dry them, then swish with oil in bowl. Don't arrange black olives against stark white foods — contrast is too sharp. Add a little catsup (or black dye) to cottage cheese, macaroni, mashed potatoes, or the like — just enough to "kill" the whiteness.

Peaches, Cling. Select halves that look soft yet have good shape, with cavity centered. Choose slices that are even in size. Leave halves in their syrup until just before using so they won't lose their life and luster. Lift out, dry lightly with towel; place white blotter underneath to absorb seepage and to reflect light through them. Brush with peach syrup just before shooting. Peach halves look best when arranged with cut side up, pit cavity showing a bit.

Peaches, Freestone. These are usually shown in

large or individual serving dishes, or in shortcakes and such desserts. Care in selecting and handling is usually sufficient.

Pears. Look for fruit of good color, firm-ripe but not hard. Play up their good definite shape, by using lengthwise pieces (halves, slices, or wedges) in arrangements. If whole Bartlett pears are used in background of pear shot, select perfect-shaped ones; let some of stems show. Handle canned pears much as directed for peaches.

Pineapple. Select slices, spears, chunks, or tidbits that have good shape and texture — not ragged, not too many white lines. For color shots pick golden-toned pieces, or tint very lightly with yellow food color (to make up for loss of delicate color in reproduction). To reflect light through it, use white paper, cut exactly to fit each piece, underneath pineapple when it is used on lettuce or parsley, or on a colored plate. (Even for an upside-down cake, pineapple pieces may be carefully lifted off and white paper inserted beneath them; then replaced, and brown sugar syrup trickled to hide mark of surgery.)

Pineapple Juice. Tint delicately if necessary. For characteristic bubbles, beat egg white slightly, and float a few on juice, using a straw or medicine dropper to transfer them.

Prunes. Cook barely tender a day ahead of time. Let stand overnight in plenty of syrup in covered dish. For stuffed prunes, don't pit — just slit them. Brush with heavy syrup for shine. If a white food is used with prunes, tint it. (See Ripe Olives, etc.)

Raisins. Plump them in boiling water before using.

Gelatin. How to make molded salads and desserts that will not slump under hot lights? Extra gelatin plus a little alum water is the answer. The results are not edible, but that is excusable in this case. These proportions work well:

For colored gelatin, add 3 envelopes of plain, unflavored gelatin to a 3-ounce package of fruit-flavored gelatin; mix thoroughly. Add 1 pint boiling water and stir till dissolved. Strain through wet cheesecloth. Stir 1 teaspoon powdered alum with

TABLEWARE

Sturdy tableware of classic design is usually more effective than fine china and linens. White or off-white is a good choice for dishes to be used in black-and-white pictures.

2 tablespoons boiling water; strain into gelatin. (If plain, uncolored gelatin is needed, soften 4 envelopes of plain unflavored gelatin in 1 pint cold water or other liquid, then stir over hot water until it dissolves. Add alum water as above. Strain before using. This jells very quickly as well as very hard, so work fast.)

If fruit, vegetables, or other salads are to be used in the mold, pour in a thin layer of the liquid gelatin; chill until barely firm; add a little more gelatin, and arrange pieces of fruit, etc., as desired. Chill. Repeat, building one layer at a time, spacing fruit to get the effect desired on surface of mold.

Miscellaneous Notes: Pour gelatin gently into mold to avoid bubbles. If you oil a mold, do so very lightly —especially when layering the gelatin. Don't let one layer harden completely before adding next one, or they may not hold together. When you turn out a mold, wipe surface with wet cotton or with fingers dipped in water. Cut white paper to fit under gelatin on plate (especially on colored plate or on lettuce), to reflect light through it, and to keep color clear and bright.

BIG QUESTION

In setting up color photographs to be used in newspapers, what colors come out best in reproduction? *Ans.* The primary colors—red, yellow, and blue. Subtle shades, fine for reproduction on high-quality paper stock, do not always come through or come true in newsprint.

Ham. Because a baked whole or half ham has such photogenic form and color, it is frequently used in pictures to dramatize other products — pineapple, peaches, glazed sweet potatoes, etc. Also, being large and recognizable, it is excellent to feature in long-shots of kitchens, dining table setups, and barbecues.

Study photographs of baked ham to determine whether you need a right or left ham to fit the proposed layout. Then shop (personally!) for one that fits both the layout and the platter to be used. (Better take platter, or paper pattern of it, with you to the meat market.)

Bake the ham (slightly under-cooked) the day before photographing, and let it stand 24 hours before cutting into it. If sliced the first day, its juices will seep out and give an unnatural iridescence to the cut surface. It is harmless, of course, but does not look right in a picture. (See "Meats" for carving notes.)

To Score and Glaze Ham. Bake ham until almost done; remove from oven. Using a strip of paper about

1¼ inches wide for a guide, cut along it (not too deeply) through fat, marking it off in strips, squares, or diamonds. To hold fat in place along edges so it won't shrink apart too much, use pins or skewers. (You may need 100 pins for a whole ham!)

Various glazes are usable. One good type is made this way: Pat sieved brown sugar evenly over fat; bake 10 minutes. Drizzle with honey; bake 10 minutes. Repeat three times. If some spots are browning too fast, cover them with bacon or pieces of foil. If not brown enough, raise ham in oven, or encourage the photographer to use a blow-torch or electric charcoal lighter (some use a chicken singeing tool) to brown it as needed.

If platter chosen is too deep to display ham well, you can fill it in either with plaster of Paris, or with cardboard matching platter in color, cut to fit exactly. Arrange garnishes to hide discrepancies — and be sure the garnishes are not too small and insignificant to be in scale with mass of ham.

Ice Cream. Real ice cream is best to use, but it does offer problems. Various photographers and art directors have their special ways of handling this product, but these suggestions may be helpful.

Have a big supply on hand, in large containers (2½ gallon size is good). Have dry ice ready, too, and kitchen tongs for handling it. If a freezing cabinet is available, fine; if not, improvise freezing "caves" from cardboard cartons (a small one inside a larger one, with dry ice between) in which to set the prepared servings.

To show the best possible flakiness of texture, scoop out the ice cream while it is semi-hard, using an ice cream spade or a big, old-fashioned kitchen spoon. This takes lots of practice, and lots of ice cream! Bed these flaky layers of ice cream on dry ice and store in freezer or cave until very hard. Arrange on a lump of dry ice in serving dish, sprinkling each layer with shaved dry ice, and rush into position before the camera. As the last grain of dry ice evaporates from the surface, the picture is snapped.

Artificial Ice Cream. This is available from Re-Lis-

GOOD TASTE

Whenever it is feasible to do so, round out the featured food with a food that complements it. In other words, make your picture "taste good." For example, with a big vegetable salad show hot rolls to take away that "raw" look. Use fresh fruit in a photo that plays up chili. Suggest hot coffee with dessert. And so on.

Tik Display Company, 811 N. Madison St., Rockford, Ill. Write them for information.

An artificial ice cream that works well for displays, and for use in some pictures, can be made by gradually beating about 1 pound of sifted powdered sugar and 2 to 3 cups fine soap flakes into 1 pound white shortening. For chocolate ice cream add cocoa with the sugar. Or color as desired. No guarantee of quality or results is supplied with this recipe!

Ice or Ice Cubes. The real thing works better than substitutes such as crumpled Cellophane.

Macaroni, Spaghetti, Noodles, and other pastes. Cook underdone. Drain, rinse, toss at once with a little oil to keep pieces from sticking together. In arranging on platter, or on top layer of casserole, etc., use fingers or tweezers to place individual strands separately, so there will be separation and definition between them.

MEATS, general. Cook roasts, steaks, chops underdone; heighten browning on fat edges and grayish spots by using blow torch or touching up with Kitchen Bouquet, or with chili powder mixed with oil.

To carve a roast without making ridges on cut surface, *press* with the knife in only one direction. Don't use sawing motion.

Hamburgers. Make extra thick.

Meat Loaf. Figure ways of breaking up flat top or sides — with garnish, or just-right sauce, or whatever. A cut meat loaf is likely to be more appealing than a solid mass.

Milk or Milky Drinks. Chief problem is to keep drinking glass clear and clean above the milk line. Solution: partially fill glass, then wait till the last minute before filling to proper line.

Nuts. Almonds ordinarily are used whole, halved, or slivered. (When chopped they lose their identity.) Blanched almonds are toasted lightly to give them a tone. Before slivering blanched almonds some experts

PLATES

Beware of plates that are too large. A piece of pie usually looks better on a bread-and-butter plate than on a pie plate. . . . Don't let foods or garnishes spill out o v e r plates' edge — keep every- t h i n g contained. . . . Don't have a lot of margin showing. . . . Plates that are definitely flat rather than "cupped" in center, work best in most cases.

like to let them dry overnight. Separate in halves, lay flat-sides down on board, and cut with French knife. Select pecan and walnut halves of good shape and color (no chips or defects), and of matching size. If chopped nuts are to be featured on frosting, etc., cut them individually on a board into good-sized pieces, then shake gently in a coarse wire strainer to get rid of fine "chaff" from cutting.

Keep the size of cookies, pieces of candy, or the like on which they are to be used in good proportion to size of nuts, so the pretty halves won't be dwarfed.

Pancakes. To make them uniform in size, dip batter with small ice cream scoop or ¼-cup measure. To keep them evenly round, cut out both ends of a shallow can of proper size (from Number 1 flat to a 1-pound shortening can). Place it on griddle, pour in batter, then remove can before edges are cooked. To achieve fine-grained, even-toned golden surface, have griddle heated just right, and don't grease it. Using too much fat causes coarse brown circles, making cakes look "fried." Cakes can be made ahead of time, stacked with waxed paper between, and frozen or refrigerated until time for photographing. Have plenty of them available for choices!

Stack cakes (or do something to them) so they won't look flat on plate. Try for different yet eatable arrangements — not so fussy that cakes in real life would surely be cold. Sausages, bacon or other meats enhance the appeal in the finished hot cake picture. Keep syrup separate unless layout demands it on the cakes. With today's fast-action lights it can be shown pouring over or dripping off a stack without too much effort.

Parsley. "A little touch of home economics," parsley has been called. Useful as it is, it should not be overused. When it is definitely needed, have on hand some that is dark green, some lighter green. One or two fairly generous spots of parsley are likely to be more effective than several smaller sprigs too evenly distributed in the composition.

If minced parsley is to be sprinkled over something,

LIGHTING

The lighting of a photograph is up to the photographer and/or art director. In general, oblique lighting (from side) is good for pictures to be used in publicity; while extra lighting at back can sometimes save retouching.

TO RESTORE PARSLEY

Have you experienced the problem of having parsley go limp — and none at hand to use? Try reviving it by clipping the stems under water. That is, fill a bowl with cold water; stand the parsley in it, and clip, clip! Leave the greens in the water until they perk up.

chop it (not too finely), then put it in a cloth or doubled paper towel and wring out the excess moisture to make it fluffy and easy to sprinkle.

PIES. Art directors and photographers always ask for a good brown rim of crust to frame the pie. (For a pie with brown filling, as pumpkin or chess, the rim may be a bit lighter.) A thicker-than-usual filling, too, is needed, and a high meringue if one is to be used.

How can an amateur make a pie shell stand up beautifully and not slump in baking? First you need a pastry that is fairly "durable," yet flaky and tender. (Proportions of 4 cups all-purpose flour to 1 cup shortening make such a crust.) Mix as usual. Don't chill the dough before rolling, but do let it stand 5 to 10 minutes. Then shape a good-sized chunk of the dough into a ball, and roll it out so it is even in thickness. Ease it into the pie pan, pushing it gently toward the center in order not to stretch it. (Stretched dough invariably shrinks while baking.) Make sure no air is trapped underneath when you press the pastry firmly against the bottom and sides of pan.

Trim edge of dough, leaving overhang as usual. Fold and press this firmly to ledge of rim before fluting it; then, as you work, bring tiny points of the dough down over edge of pan, to "lock" each fluting in place. Prick bottom and sides generously, then chill thoroughly before baking.

Before putting the crust into the oven cut a square or circle of foil and press gently into the unbaked shell, letting edges extend up above the rim. Fill this foil lining clear to the top with uncooked rice. Bake in a hot oven (450° or 475°) until rim begins to look cooked but not brown. Remove from oven, spoon out some of the rice, then lift out foil and all. (Save rice — it can be used over and over in pie shells, or cooked and eaten.) Prick shell again and put back to finish baking. Watch it! If rim shows signs of browning too fast, use a long band of foil around outside of pan, bending top edge to protect rim. If crust balloons up in spots, prick it with a sharp fork. If it puffs up around the bottom, press it gently back into place with cloth or paper towel.

LATTICE TOP FOR PIE

Weave the strips of pastry on waxed paper on a baking sheet; freeze. It's easy then to slide it onto the pie and, after a few minutes' thawing, to finish the rim as usual.

Double-crust pies offer fewer difficulties, but do require almost constant watching during baking, and use of pieces of foil to control browning.

To Cut and Serve Pie. Cut edges of crust first, with razor blade. Then cut top crust with small sharp knife held vertically. After cutting, separate flakes slightly with tip of knife to play up the texture. To cut meringue, use razor blade, scissors, wet knife — or combination of these. (A tender meringue helps most!) To display a piece of pie, use a bread-and-butter size plate rather than a salad or pie size, so it will show off to advantage. To hold up that outer crust on the cut piece, cut a wedge out of a foil pie pan and slip it under the piece of pie. It won't show in the picture, for the point of a piece of pie is always toward the camera.

For Action Pictures. To get contrast, use a pale blue canvas or board for rolling out crust for television, or action picture in black and white. Or use yellow shortening or tint the dough yellow.

Puddings, Soft Type. Lay piece of waxed paper or foil on surface of pudding while it cools, to prevent a skin from forming. Stir or beat gently just before spooning into dessert dishes so it will look glossy. Heap it in soft mounds for height, or swirls for texture. Decorate top if it looks too plain: a fluff of whipped cream, a walnut half, or dash of chopped nuts, or other appropriate garnish. Work extra hard for design in the composition of the picture.

Salads and Dressings. Strive for form in salads. Use big pieces, not finely chopped mixtures. Even a bowl of lettuce or mixed greens can have form and design — never a haphazard, blowzy look! Use some light, some dark green lettuce, plus tomato wedges, egg quarters, onion rings, or something of the sort to contribute design to the top.

To achieve smartly simple design on plate or platter salads, use greens sparingly, particularly for black and white pictures. Plain plates with definite shapes and simple edges are usually best; medium-dark for light salads, lighter plates for dark-toned ones.

SLIDES AND FILMS

Remember that food set-ups that will be projected on a screen will make objects appear over-large. For that reason, it is well to select tableware with short handles and to place it so that it is not over-prominent in the picture.

Dressings are usually shown separately, in bowl or bottle. To fill a bottle with creamy dressing without splattering it inside, use a funnel. (For a very deep bottle, you can improvise a long funnel by removing the bulb from a suction baster!) If using mayonnaise or similar thick dressing, have it well chilled, and put it on the salad at the last minute.

Sandwiches. Design in the sandwiches and pattern in their arrangement are important. For handling small tea sandwiches, follow suggestions under "Cookies." Using toasted English muffins as a base for sandwich or creamed food? Don't split them in exact halves. (They'll look too flat.) About three-fourths the height is better.

Soup. Use interesting dishes — cups, mugs, bowls. Break up flat surface with a touch of floating garnish. To make oysters, vegetables, etc., stay up so they will show, use a disk of clear plastic under surface of soup to support them.

Tea. Use the real thing. Iced tea? See "Ice Cubes."

Turkey. Roast turkey looks much more natural and appetizing in a picture when it is not really roasted. Some expert home economists simply massage the turkey all over with peanut oil mixed with soy sauce or Kitchen Bouquet, then put it on its back — not on a V-rack — in a shallow pan and heat in slow oven 30 to 60 minutes, or until the skin looks translucent and "cooked." Brush occasionally with the oil-soy sauce mixture. Watch carefully; if a spot browns quickly, lay a piece of foil over it. (Some photographers like to use a blow torch, or an electric charcoal lighter, to brown skin as desired.)

STYROFOAM

A pointed saw is a good tool to use for cutting styrofoam a desired shape.

VEGETABLES. To "cook" most fresh or frozen vegetables for pictures, simply cover with boiling water, drain almost immediately, run cold water over them, then immerse in cold water or mineral oil to keep them from discoloring, shriveling, or "dimpling" as green peas do. (Frozen ones sometimes need only to be thawed in cold water.)

Beets and red cabbage come out dark purple in color photographs. (For pickled beet slices, turnip slices dyed a slightly lighter red can be used; reproduced, they look more naturalistic than real beets ever would.)

Showing creamed vegetable on a plate? Give shape to the composition somehow — with toast points, or whatever inspiration suggests. (Save out some of the uncreamed vegetable to poke in here and there on top, so it will register.) Plain cooked vegetables require careful arranging.

TEST

By using a Polaroid camera, is it possible for the home economist to tell in advance how c e r t a i n colors will show up when photographed in black and white? Yes, to some extent. Much depends, however, on how the photographer lights the final setup. Under some lighting a shade of blue can come through dark, while with other lighting it will look pale.

Potatoes. Use a touch of black dye in mashed potatoes to give them tone in reproduction. For baked potatoes, don't oil the skins. Baking at 450° for 30 minutes, then at 350° until done results in fluffy interior without over-browning skin.

Tomatoes. Whether a tomato will be firm and solid, or watery and holey inside cannot be confidently guessed from the outside — but shaking the tomato is something of a test. If it rattles when shaken, it's watery! But play safe and buy plenty, even if you need only one. For color pictures, rich, ripe red tomatoes are best; for black-and-white, choose a medium-light color. To ripen tomatoes, store in a dark cupboard for two or three days.

For stuffed tomatoes, whether baked or salad-filled, turn tomato stem-end down. For such specialties as a baked tomato topped with mayonnaise puff, cook the tomato and the puff separately, then combine.

Wines. Use simple, undecorated glasses, preferably tulip-shaped. To open bottles, cut (don't tear) the foil or cellulose band ¼-inch below lip; wipe lip. Remove cork (jackknife corkscrew is excellent); wipe lip again. Red wines look inky if not diluted. For red table wines use about half wine, half water. For port, use one-third water. Fill glasses about ⅔ full; remove bubbles. Lighting is highly important — but the photographer is aware of that!

Personal Postscript From the Authors

IN THIS NEW EDITION of *How To Write for Homemakers*, our aim has been to pin-point fundamental facts, and, at the same time, to needle your thinking! We have tried to restate basic principles in new ways, just as you in Clothing and Textiles restate basic dress design in fresh, new fashions.

Now the book is done, and we come to the index. Here we ask ourselves: "Shall we make this index look and read like every other index, or shall we rethink it and, perhaps, restyle it to give these last pages a custom-made look that fits the spirit of the book?"

In making the decision, our figuring went something like this: Surely everyone who reads or examines this book knows that a chapter on recipe writing would logically cover the arrangement of ingredients in a recipe, so why list the word *Ingredients* in the index? (Anyone concerned would be much more likely to look under *Recipes;* much more likely to read the entire chapter on that subject.) However, a reader or prospective reader is entitled to find a word such as *Copyrights* listed, for she has no way of knowing in which chapter or under what heading copyrights are discussed. Proceeding along this line of thought, we have shortened and sharpened as needed to interpret what is in the book.

We do not mean to convey the idea that this is an ideal index pattern for all books. Far from it. For example, a cookbook that is not completely cross-indexed is of little value. We do believe, however, in ever looking at the world of words with fresh eyes. Including indexes!

So much for our reasoning. Whatever your reactions to it or to other phases of the book, we shall appreciate hearing from you. After all, it *is* a book of Communications, you know! — G.A.C. and L.R.

Interpretive Index